Kari Polanyi Levitt and Canadian Political Economy

Michèle Rioux · Hughes Brisson

Kari Polanyi Levitt and Canadian Political Economy

palgrave
macmillan

Michèle Rioux
Université du Québec à Montréal
Montréal, QC, Canada

Hughes Brisson
Université du Québec à Montréal
Montréal, QC, Canada

ISBN 978-3-030-87363-9 ISBN 978-3-030-87364-6 (eBook)
https://doi.org/10.1007/978-3-030-87364-6

This Palgrave Macmillan imprint is published by the registered company Springer Nature Switzerland AG
The registered company address is: Gewerbestrasse 11, 6330 Cham, Switzerland

To Kari
And to my children, Théa and Sid Donarski

Foreword

This delightful book pays tribute to a distinguished economist and wonderful human being, Kari Polanyi Levitt, who at time of publication will be entering her 99th year.

It is my personal privilege to have known Kari for about four decades and to have made an unfailing practice of taking her for dinner near her Montréal home on every visit to that city in recent years. These meetings—full of life and informed talk on economics and economists, on politics, society, and history—have had on me the same effect, as I believe they must have had on all of her many friends.

It is through Kari that I first became aware of the central role of Afro-Caribbean slavery in the origins of capitalism—one of the many gaps in my education and in my teaching that she has helped to close. We have deeper connections, especially to our teacher Nicholas Kaldor and to others of the Cambridge circle with whom we studied, although three decades apart. And we share, of course, a bond of responsibility for the legacies of our fathers, a far heavier duty in her case than mine, which she has executed with grace and skill for nearly half a century.

Readers who have encountered Kari only through her scholarship will find here the full story of this remarkable woman. It begins with her childhood in Red Vienna, continues through her education in London and work on strategic bombing, and eventuates in her professional life in Canada, in the Caribbean, and in world economics, to which her clear mind and critical voice have made exceptional contributions. Throughout, there runs the thread of devotion to her extraordinary parents.

Kari combines the essential traits of a great economist, of which, let me argue, there are four. The first is a deep education in both the history of economic ideas and the history of economies proper, embedding the strictly economic in the social dimension. The second is the will, the ability, and the patience to bring evidence to bear—including statistics, history, and the observation of the eyes and ears. The third is a keen sense of what is vital for policy, as economics is a policy discipline, and if it is not political and policy-oriented, it is nothing at all. And fourth, perhaps most difficult to acquire and to maintain, is a critical independence from the orthodoxies that academic economists embrace, in order to enjoy an untroubled life.

How Kari Polanyi Levitt came to possess these traits, thanks to Michèle Rioux and Hugues Brisson, you are about to learn.

Bonne lecture!

Austin, Texas
May 2021

James K. Galbraith

Tribute, by Margie Mandell

Tribute to Kari Polanyi Levitt

Marguerite (Margie) Mendell, Director, Karl Polanyi Institute of Political Economy, Concordia University, Montreal.

It is a pleasure and an honor for me to pay tribute to my friend and colleague Kari Polanyi Levitt. Currently Professor Emerita, Economics, McGill University. Kari Polanyi Levitt's distinguished career spans more than six decades of teaching, mentoring, research, publications, establishing and nurturing networks of scholarly exchange and actively participating in critical public debates in Canada and abroad. She has taught generations of students in economic development and political economy in Canada and in the Caribbean, many of whom are distinguished academics and public figures today.

Professor Polanyi Levitt was born in Vienna, Austria, the daughter of Karl Polanyi and Ilona Duczynska. I have had the privilege of long conversations over many years with Kari Polanyi Levitt about her childhood in Vienna, about the leading intellectuals and public figures who frequented the Polanyi home until the rising tide of fascism forced her father to emigrate to England with his daughter, Kari. It was in wartime England that Kari Polanyi studied at the LSE with some of the most eminent economists at the time. After graduation in 1947, she emigrated to Canada where she married, had two sons, Tom and Harry, and received a Master's Degree in Economics from the University of Toronto. She accepted an appointment in the Department of Economics at McGill University in 1961, where she taught until her retirement in 1992.

I will only share with you some of Professor Polanyi Levitt's numerous accomplishments, engagements, and contributions. In the 1960s, she advised governments on the creation of National Accounts in Trinidad and Tobago and Haiti, and produced an extensive report for the government of Canada on its relations with the Caribbean. In 1970, the publication of her book, **Silent Surrender: The Multinational Corporation,** equipped those arguing against the domination of the Canadian economy by multinationals with extensive documentation and rigorous analysis. Her research was at the core of political debates on foreign ownership at the time and influenced the creation of the Foreign Investment Review Agency by the Government of Canada in 1973, with a mandate to screen foreign acquisitions of Canadian businesses and to advise government on actions to be taken. In 2008, Kari Polanyi Levitt was awarded the *John Kenneth Galbraith Prize* with Professor Mel Watkins for their contribution to Canadian political economy and to progressive economics. *Silent Surrender* was later translated into French as *La capitulation tranquille*. It was reissued in 2001 and is a classic in Canadian political economy.

Kari Polanyi Levitt has inspired many students in Canada and abroad over several decades. As a former student of hers in the 1970s, I recall her seminars that went overtime because no one wished to leave and the summer reading courses she generously led on a voluntary basis with several of us interested in deepening our knowledge of development economics and in particular, the writings of Latin American economists at the time. I recall those day long discussions, usually in someone's garden and yes, I recall the enjoyable meals and the wine in between. Always committed to social justice, she instilled in her students the need to nuance, to deepen our understanding of the complexities of political and economic challenges in developed and developing countries that could only be understood and approached with a broad analytical framework and a critical eye.

Professor Polanyi Levitt's steadfast commitment to open dialogue and debate in economics, her insistence on the need to understand the theoretical debates that have shaped economic theory historically, challenged the narrow perspective that overtook the profession in the 1980s and the marginalization of economic development, economic history, history of economic thought, and comparative perspectives. So as to institutionalize development studies, she co-founded the *Canadian Association for the Study of International Development* (CASID) in the early 1980s. CASID now awards an annual *Kari Polanyi Levitt Prize* to the best original essay by a graduate student in international development studies. Kari Polanyi Levitt encouraged young economists to pursue their interest in economic development theory during the many years when the field was marginalized by the economics profession. Her work and her support for talented young economists have contributed to the renaissance of economic development theory and to reclaiming its place in economics. Among her many honors, she was awarded an *Honorary Doctorate from The University of the West Indies* in 2008 in recognition of her contribution to international development, her teaching, publications, and participation in public life in the Caribbean over several decades.

It was in the early 1980s that Kari Polanyi Levitt invited me to collaborate with her on the life and work of her father, Karl Polanyi. She wished to organize her father's archive, a project begun earlier by her late mother. Our collaboration of more than three decades is a story unto itself. The reading, discussing, sorting, cataloguing, debating, and marveling at what we discovered describe our experience throughout these years, and it continues today.

Kari Polanyi Levitt invited the Hungarian Academy of Sciences to host an international Karl Polanyi conference in Budapest in 1986, marking the centenary of his birth. Academics from numerous countries and disciplines gathered in Budapest to discuss the work of Karl Polanyi. Participants expressed their desire to pursue the conversation begun in Budapest. In 1987, with the encouragement of two colleagues at Concordia, the late Dr. Charles Bertrand, Dean of the Faculty of Arts and Sciences at the time, and Professor Daniel Shapiro from the Department of Economics and the School of Community and Public Affairs, the Karl Polanyi Institute was established at Concordia University and became the repository of the Karl Polanyi Archive, Polanyi's literary legacy. The newly created Institute hosted the second international Karl Polanyi conference at Concordia in 1988. Unexpectedly, the COVID pandemic meant that our 15th international conference held recently in April 2021 was entirely virtual.

I will not go on about the work of the Institute but wish to share with you the commitment that Kari Polanyi Levitt has had and continues to have to the widest possible dissemination of her father's ideas. The Institute has played this role for more than three decades, with the archive as its centerpiece, its crown jewel, an archive that has been consulted by faculty, students, activists, public intellectuals, and journalists, representing many disciplines and organizations from all over the world, generating numerous publications across disciplines and public spaces, including several important books on the life and work of Karl Polanyi. Kari Polanyi Levitt has given pubic lectures and keynote addresses at international conferences and published extensively on the significance of her father's work drawing upon her deep knowledge and expertise as an eminent economist who has engaged with the most important debates in the latter part of the twentieth century and into the twenty-first century. Her insight into the work of her father has contributed to a better understanding of the roots of his work in Europe from the turn of the twentieth century until his death in 1964, to the significance of his ideas in the history of political economy and to the widespread and growing recognition of the resonance of his work to contemporary debates.

I would like to quote from the foreword to the Mexican edition of her book, *From the Great Transformation to the Great Financialization*, by Harvard economist, Dani Rodrik:

> *Perhaps no-one has greater claim to the mantle of keeping Karl Polanyi's thought vibrant and relevant to our current problems than Kari Polanyi Levitt herself. In this beautifully written collection of essays, she not only draws a vivid portrait of her father as a man, a scholar, and an activist, but also provides some extraordinarily prescient analysis of how the world economy got to where it is today. Levitt's memories of her father are particularly touching. In addition, the essays range widely over economic history, the history of economic thought, the international economic system, and economic development. They are all informed by the same combination of sharp insight and social conscience that made Karl Polanyi's work stand out. Levitt brings a rich historical texture to the analysis of contemporary problems of the global economy and the challenges of economic development. The spirit of Polanyi lurks always, not too far from the surface.*

Professor Polanyi Levitt's generosity is the source of the Institute's achievements. She has opened the access to her father's rich literary legacy without reservation. The digitalization of the Archive has, I believe, fulfilled her wish to make her father's work as widely and as easily available as possible. She has tirelessly worked with me and with Ana Gomez on organizing international conferences both here at Concordia and at universities abroad. Her active participation in discussions on the work of her father, her commitment to a public space for reflection and debate inspired by her father's work, and her publications and public lectures on the resonance of Karl Polanyi's work to contemporary issues and challenges, are at the heart of the Institute and its ongoing work.

I conclude on a personal note by thanking Kari for inviting me on this intellectual journey more than thirty years ago and for her precious collaboration and friendship. It has been an honor and a joy to work with you Kari and to have your trust, friendship, and respect all these years. I wish to congratulate Michèle Rioux and Hughes Brisson for this book dedicated to the life and work of Kari Polanyi Levitt and for inviting me to pay tribute to her. As we know, Kari Polanyi Levitt has been unable to physically participate in events for the last two years. Her health no longer permits her to move about but for those of us close to her, we can attest to her remarkable intellectual energy and commitment to continue her engagement with the challenges of our times, especially in the face of the pandemic and what this crisis means for the future of democracy and social justice, her lifelong commitments. Kari Polanyi Levitt's vitality is remarkable and it has meant that I can continue to enjoy the privilege of close friendship, collaboration, and the inspiration. I have drawn from Kari since the early 1970s when I was her graduate student. Thank you Kari for your companionship and generosity. Thank you Michèle and Hughes for inviting me to write this tribute to an extraordinary woman, a fierce intellectual and great humanitarian.

Marguerite Mendell
Distinguished Professor Emerita,
Director
School of Community and Public
Affairs, Karl Polanyi Institute
of Political Economy
Concordia University
Montreal, QC, Canada

Contents

1	**Introduction**	1
	References	6
2	**The Trajectory of a Lifetime Part 1: From Red Vienna to London**	7
	Red Vienna	8
	Kari Polanyi at the London School of Economics	12
	First Steps in the World of Work	17
	References	19
3	**Trajectory of Life, Part 2: Crossing the Ocean to Canada and the Caribbean**	21
	Back to Graduate Studies: Passion for Development Studies and Early Recruitment by McGill University	26
	Silent Surrender: Canada as a Developed Dependent Country	29
	Caribbean Life: The Emergence of the Plantation Economy Model	33
	References	40
4	**The Trajectory of Life Part 3—A Retirement and Her father's Legacy. And Beyond?**	43
	The Legacy of Her Father	45

And Beyond 48
References 51

5 Conclusion 53

Postface 59

Timeline 63

Bibliography 67

List of Figures

Fig. 2.1	Kari, 1930–31	10
Fig. 2.2	Kari and her father Karl Polanyi in 1939	11
Fig. 2.3	Kari at LSE, 1941–42	12
Fig. 2.4	Kari at LSE, 1941–42	14
Fig. 3.1	Kari—Editor of the Mine & Mill Herald—Toronto (mid 1950s)	22
Fig. 3.2	Kari—Electoral campaign and Editor Mine & Mill Herald—Toronto	22
Fig. 3.3	Kari 1952—With son Tom and Karl Polanyi	23
Fig. 3.4	1949, Labour Day Toronto	23
Fig. 3.5	Kari, Joe Levitt with friend (New York, 1947)	24
Fig. 3.6	Kari with her mother Ilona Duczynska (donation of artworks to Poland, belonging to Ilona's family, dating back to the nineteenth century)	25
Fig. 3.7	1957—Kari and Karl (Ontario)	26
Fig. 3.8	Kari in Trinidad	34
Fig. 3.9	End of 60s, with her sons Tom and Harry	40
Fig. 4.1	Kari, Early 1980s	44
Fig. 4.2	Kari when the ashes of her parents were returned to Budapest, 1983	46
Fig. 5.1	Kari in Haiti, 1986	54
Fig. 5.2	Kari at her Book Launch, University of Jamaica, 2010	54

CHAPTER 1

Introduction

Abstract Kari Polanyi Levitt is an influential figure of Canadian political economy and economic development. This book traces her life trajectory and discusses her scientific contributions. It offers scholars and the public interested in political economy a panorama of social and economic policy changes of the last century that are related to the story of her intellectual life.

Keywords Canadian · Political economy · Development studies · Economic development · Canadian influential women

M. Rioux and H. Brisson, *Kari Polanyi Levitt and Canadian Political Economy*, https://doi.org/10.1007/978-3-030-87364-6_1

Kari Polanyi Levitt, Emerita Professor of Economics, McGill University, Montréal Québec, Canada

Kari Levitt was born in Vienna in 1923, first and only child of Karl Polanyi and Ilona Duczynska. Kari attended Bedales School (1936-1942) and the London School of Economics (1942 – 1947). She graduated from LSE with First Class Honours, specializing in statistics. In 1957, Kari returned to graduate studies in economics at the University of Toronto. From 1965 until 1975, she directed a major project of construction of input-output tables for the Atlantic Provinces of Canada, at Statistics Canada. In the 1980s, Kari was occupied with the responsibility of the literary legacy of Karl Polanyi which passed to her on the death of her mother, Ilona, in 1978. In 1987, Concordia University accepted a proposal by Dr. Marguerite Mendell to establish the Karl Polanyi Institute of Political Economy and Professor Levitt made the Polanyi archive available. She retired from McGill in 1992 as Emerita Professor. She was able to concentrate her efforts on teaching and research at the University of the West Indies in Jamaica until 1997. In recent years, Kari returned to an incomplete manuscript on theories of economic development.

Source: Personal website Kari Polanyi Levitt (http://www.karipolanyilevitt.com)

Kari Polanyi Levitt is an influential figure of Canadian political economy and economic development. At the heart of her thinking is an incessant quest for the redistribution of wealth and social justice, both of which have become increasingly important in today's world since power is more concentrated, whether economic or political, and inequalities are growing. This book traces her life trajectory, which spans almost a century (1923–), and discusses her scientific contributions.

As a woman, she was able to shine in a discipline dominated by men, with significant contributions on economic and political debates in Canada and abroad since the late 1960s. In Canada, her ideas have influenced debates on the role of institutions and economic policies. Abroad, she has been a critical thinker of economic development. Her perspectives on the transformation of the world economy since the end of the Second World War are still very pertinent. She believes in the intervention of the state in the economy to achieve social justice and economic development. Her critical perspective reminds us that the international economic order has changed as neoliberal thinking has gained influence since the 1970s. Neoliberalism shifted toward competition and trade liberalization, thereby shifting the burden of adjustment to workers and developing countries. In contrast, the ideas and principles at the core of the international economic order erected after 1945 were strongly influenced by John Maynard Keynes. State interventionism and international cooperation were at the center of instruments created to stabilize the economy, to support economic development, and to achieve full employment. In parallel, international development and cooperation were geared toward stimulating growth in developing countries to rebalance international economic relations and terms of trade.

Influenced by Marx and Keynes, and by her father, Karl Polanyi, her scientific contributions made her a reference in Canada. The excellence of her publications allowed her to obtain prestigious positions and multiple honors. As of 2021, at 97 years old, Kari Polanyi Levitt is still an active researcher, continues to publish and, in 2019 attended conferences around the world, from Seoul to Vienna, to Cuba, Trinidad, and Mexico, where she still communicated her ideas.

In 1934, as the daughter of the famous Hungarian economist, Karl Polanyi, she witnessed the repression of the worker's movement in Vienna. Four years before the arrival of the Nazi regime in Austria, this crackdown announced the end of the Austrian socialist movement which had dominated the politics of Red Vienna for more than a decade. Later, as a refugee in England during the war, she studied economics at the London School of Economics while attending meetings of the London Marxist circles. She later became a professor at McGill University where she worked on the development of statistical tools for the design of economic policies for the Maritime provinces, as well as international development.

She is known for having published *Silent Surrender* which dealt with the consequences of the massive investments of US multinationals in Canada during the 1960s. The book, a classic of Canadian economic literature, was reissued in 2002 enriched with a new introduction and a preface by Mel Watkins. During the second half of the 1970s, she contributed to the development of the theory of plantation economics which introduced colonialism and slave trade in the study of Caribbean political economy. This was important since it broke from the dominant theoretical models coming from the developed world, which did not consider the social, historical, and cultural particularities of Caribbean countries.

At the death of her mother in 1978, she became responsible for keeping the archives of her father, Karl Polanyi. This facilitated a dialogue between her and the work of her father that has affected her publications in the last two decades. Most recently, Kari Polanyi Levitt has written on the lack of regulation of the global economy and the weakness of state intervention since the 2008 financial crisis. She cast a doubt over the ability of the globalized economy to promote stability, innovation, and full employment. First and foremost, she fears that globalization will increasingly benefit only a few at the expense of the improvement of the lives of the many. According to her, we must actively seek more progressive outcomes to promote a balanced globalization. The quest for social justice was always an underlying theme of her academic teaching and research.[1] Throughout her life, her critical thinking denounced the individualism that characterizes contemporary societies. She preferred regulated markets with an eye in the public interest rather than having unregulated markets ruling over the public interest.

[1] The contributions of Kari Polanyi Levitt transcend the discipline of economics, taking into account the interactions between the different spheres of life inherent in the globalization process and capitalism.

She thought in scientific and pragmatic terms thanks to her passion for statistics and mathematics. She distanced herself early on from structuralist and deterministic approaches, which she considered disconnected from social practices aimed at social justice (Mendell 2005). Cameron (2005) recalled that the work of Kari Polanyi Levitt was marked by an urgency and an ability to analyze and resolve "invisible" but concrete daily problems and to actually render them "visible."

This book is about meeting Kari. Two professors I had studied with at Glendon College, York University, Omar Hamouda and Lori Tarshis, a student of Keynes, had encouraged me to contact Kari Polanyi Levitt when I relocated to Montréal in 1987. I first met her at McGill in a graduate seminar on Development Economics. Kari Polanyi Levitt appeared as one of the most inspiring women in Canadian and international political economy. As a professor of political economy at UQAM since 2006, I felt a desire to know more about her work and life to be able to discuss her scientific contribution with my students. Hugues was one of the assistants that I suggested to Kari to help her with her research work. Kari had a problem with reading and needed assistants. This is how Hughes Brisson has been involved in the project of this book since its very beginning.

This publication is based on interviews with her and some of her colleagues organized between 1989 and 2020,[2] the analytical reading of her works, and a review of the literature. We planned interviews, meetings, dinners, and brunches to document and analyze Kari's life and contribution to political economy; especially, the political economy of the decentered communities and regions of the world. It offers scholars and the public interested in political economy a panorama of social and economic policy changes of the last century that are related to the story of her intellectual life. Information boxes provide background information on important authors and concepts that are mentioned throughout. This helps put into perspective our humble contribution to the documentation of her passion for political economy and to understand her contribution to empower societies and promote development.[3]

We would like to thank Kari for her generosity in sharing her understanding of the world and how we can understand how the world works,

[2] Rioux and Brisson (2012).

[3] After years of organizing a voluminous set of correspondence and texts, these archives are available to the public thanks to the Karl Polanyi Institute of Political Economy at Concordia University in Montreal.

evolves, and changes. Her passion for facts, statistics, and history is inspiring, since they can help us understand the world and to make it a better place for all. We also thank Philippe Langlois for his valuable research and comments, James Galbraith who so kindly accepting to write the preface of this book, Marguerite Mandell who wrote a great and warm tribute and Angélique Willkie who provided a Postface.[4]

References

Cameron, Duncan. 2005. 'Epilogue.' In *Reclaiming Democracy: The Social Justice and Political Economy of Gregory Baum and Kari Polanyi Levitt*, edited by Marguerite Mendell, 167–174. Montreal: McGill-Queen's University Press.

Mendell, Marguerite. 2005. *Reclaiming Democracy: The Social Justice and Political Economy of Gregory Baum and Kari Polanyi Levitt*. Montreal: McGill-Queen's University Press.

Rioux, Michèle, and Hughes Brisson. 2012. 'Interview with Kari Levitt: "Bring the State Back In!".' *Revue Interventions économiques* 45: 12–18. Accessed April 21, 2021. http://interventionseconomiques.revues.org/1686.

[4] We acknowledge the financial support of the Faculté de science politique et de droit de l'Université du Québec à Montréal, the FRQSC (Fonds de recherche du Québec—Société et culture) and the SSHRC (Social Science and Humanities Research Council). We also thank Sid Donarski for assistance in translation and edition.

CHAPTER 2

The Trajectory of a Lifetime Part 1: From Red Vienna to London

Abstract Kari Polanyi's youth is recounted, from her youth in Vienna in the 1920s to her years in London, where she studied at LSE, made her first steps as a young scholar in economics, and worked in a worker's union. This chapter shines a light on what influenced Kari Polanyi during this first part of her life: her parents (Karl Polanyi, Ilona Duczynska); Red Vienna; working for a major union of war industry workers; as well as economists Kaldor, Kalecki, Keynes, Marx, Arthur Lewis, Raúl Prebisch, and Celso Furtado.

Keywords Red Vienna · Karl Polanyi · London School of Economics · Development studies · Influence of Keynes on Economic Thought

As Kari Polanyi Levitt recognizes similarities that unite people of the world as well as the richness of national, local, and individual differences, she is a true "Citizen of the world." She traveled extensively and lived in many parts of the world, from pre-fascist Austria to England at war; then to Canada; and many times to the Caribbean. She changed trajectory many times and experienced a diversity of human and social environments. A thread links her path: her desire to contribute to the construction of a better world based on the principle of social justice and scientific research.

M. Rioux and H. Brisson, *Kari Polanyi Levitt and Canadian Political Economy*, https://doi.org/10.1007/978-3-030-87364-6_2

Red Vienna

> I was born in Vienna, shortly after the end of the First World War. It was a chaotic and economically very difficult time. My father, Karl Polanyi, then in his forties, had a good position as a journalist for an important weekly economic and financial journal. My mother was studying engineering. I had a very happy childhood, even though I was the only child. Growing up in Red Vienna was perhaps the most successful illustration of what a socialist urban government can achieve in a country that was quite poor, with a high rate of unemployment. Production did not reach the prewar level until 1928. Socialist governments were elected from the revolution of 1918, which put an end to the Austro-Hungarian monarchy until the overthrow of the working-class movement in February 1934. Red Vienna had remarkable housing projects, of which the Karl Marx Hof was the best known but there were dozens, if not hundreds of them. The defining moment of my life was when the working-class movement was attacked. (Interview[1])

The political context that existed in Red Vienna had a great impact on her life. At the end of the First World War, which ended the Austro-Hungarian Empire in place since 1867, everything had to be rebuilt. Vienna was then led by a social democratic coalition that attracted intellectuals, numerous artists, and socialist activists wishing to participate in the construction of a new social project. Becoming a major hub in Central Europe, Vienna then experienced unprecedented excitement, both culturally and politically. The Austrian capital was called "Red Vienna" between 1918 and 1934. This first democratically elected government in the territory of the former Habsburg empire became a laboratory for social policy and some of its political innovations were very successful at influencing the rest of Europe during the twentieth century. Policies included the introduction of an eight-hour workday and the establishment of an unemployment insurance system.

Kari Polanyi's parents had left Hungary to settle in Vienna where they quickly felt at home. Karl Polanyi contributed through his editorials to

[1] All quotations in this book are from direct interviews with Kari Polanyi Levitt. Interviews with the authors at Kari Polanyi Levitt's apartment, December 27 and 30, 2011; Interview with the authors at UQAM, November 12, 2012. Interview with the authors at Kari Polanyi Levitt's apartment, October 20, 2013.

discussions surrounding the construction of social democratic administrations. Vienna was fertile ground for Karl Polanyi, a young intellectual who succeeded in making his place in the Viennese press. Her mother, Ilona Duczynska, was actively involved in the Communist Party. She had taken part in the revolution that took place in Budapest in 1918, while working for the government of the brief Hungarian Soviet Republic led by Bela Kun before being accused of high treason.

> My parents are very different from each other. My father worked in the area of ideas and my mother was an activist. As a young woman, she played an important role in the Hungarian struggle against the First World War. She became a national heroic figure together with her comrade and first husband in organizing the production of anti-war literature distributed in the war factories and army barracks of Budapest. She was arrested and accused of treason. My mother has been described as a sovereign revolutionary; she was no camp follower. I admired my mother. When I was young, she was my model, rather than my father. It was much later in life that I grew to appreciate the ideas of my father. Both my parents had an influence and I always felt, because of growing up in a socialist household, in a socialist Red Vienna, that I had to put the education that I had received and whatever natural intelligence I had been endowed with in some way to use in this world. Wherever I found myself, I would become engaged in a positive way, in an effort to serve a cause. It stems from the prevailing values of my family. The other thing is curiosity, I am extremely curious.

The beginning of the 1930s marked the end of this golden age of socialism in Vienna. As early as 1933, following the suspension of the Austrian parliament and Hitler's coming to power, the newspaper for which Polanyi wrote, the *Österreichische Volkswirt*, could no longer keep a left-wing editorialist in its ranks.

> I was 10 years old. The Austrian government destroyed the working-class movement in Vienna. There was to be a general strike. On my way to school, I noticed that the electric clock in the public square had stopped and I knew that this was the beginning of the strike. My mother told me that she would be busy for the next few days and that I would be in charge of the house and of the care of my grandmother. I was given, for the first time, paper money. I went down to buy a lot of bread and made all kinds of preparations for these few days. Because we lived rather near to the barracks, we could see the army bring their guns to bombard the

social housing. I think this was the defining moment of my life because I knew which side I was on, the side of the workers of Vienna. I remained concerned with political events for the next ten years, twenty years or maybe eighty years. The civil war lasted four days and the government won. The leaders of the social democratic party left the country. I went back to school, but half of the teachers were gone. They were dismissed because they were socialists. I was sent to England on a train.

The Polanyi family emigrated to London, England. Karl Polanyi, who left first, worked with the *Workers Education Association* in adult education, affiliated with the universities of London and Oxford. In 1934, Kari joined her father in London and the family was reunited in 1936 (Fig. 2.1).

Fig. 2.1 Kari, 1930–31

BOX Karl Polanyi Karl Polanyi was an Economist of Austrian origin who grew up in Hungary. He is recognized as an outstanding thinker of the twentieth century. His most important work *The Great Transformation*, published in 1944, explained the rise of fascism in the twentieth century as well as the way in which the market economy imposed itself as an ideological project idealizing the self-regulating potential of the market. Polanyi observed the development of capitalism in the nineteenth century and argued that the emergence of a market society marked a historic break: For the first time, the economy prevailed over the other institutions of society. Once the economic sphere is empowered, social relationships lose their anchor in all other social spheres and become devoid of humanity. The market is not an ahistorical mechanism for regulating trade, this is a liberal utopia. This aspiration for utopia explained the abuses of fascism because of the conflict between having self-regulating markets and protecting the populations. In his later work, Polanyi examined non-capitalist societies and developed his institutionalist perspective. Different institutions are interconnected in a specific arrangement in each society and era, revealing the prevalent norms in each society at a certain time. Looking at the changing relationships between society and the economy (Maucourant and Plociniczak 2011), Karl Polanyi stressed that political and religious institutions have always governed economic relations and that the primacy of the economic sphere in our contemporary societies represented a historical exception.

To learn more about the life of Karl Polanyi: Maucourant (2011); Dale (2016); Dale (2015); Polanyi Levitt (1990a). To better understand

Fig. 2.2 Kari and her father Karl Polanyi in 1939

Polanyi's thought: Dale (2010); Dale (2016); McRobbie and Polanyi Levitt (2000); Clancier et al. (2005). Also visit the website of the Karl Polanyi Institute of Political Economy at https://www.concordia.ca/research/polanyi.html (Fig. 2.2).

Kari Polanyi at the London School of Economics

> Arriving in England was a challenge. I went to stay with very close family friends and learned English within a year or two. I was fortunate to have a very good education because I won a scholarship to a prestigious avant-garde boarding school. I was always reading. (Fig. 2.3)

In 1941, as the Second World War had been raging for two years, Kari Polanyi went to university. Interested in physics and history, she applied

Fig. 2.3 Kari at LSE, 1941–42

to various universities in these disciplines. She was happy to be admitted to Cambridge in physics, but with no scholarship. She was accepted at Oxford in history, but with no scholarship. These refusals were difficult for her to accept. She applied to the London School of Economics (LSE) where fees were less prohibitive and chose to specialize in statistics to take advantage of her passion for mathematics.

> At this time, my father was in the United States and my mother had joined him. I refused to leave England and I was living with friends. I tried for physics at Cambridge and was accepted into the second year of the program but with no scholarship. I decided that I was an academic failure. I followed my political left- wing interests at LSE that was temporarily relocated to Cambridge where we could attend lectures by any of the famous Cambridge economists, Joan Robinson and others, as well as our own lecturers.

LSE proved to be a great environment for her. During these years, the government, in search of appropriate economic policies in the context of the war, actively sought the services of economists, notably among the teachers at LSE. Polanyi was fortunate enough to have as teachers promising young economists who would mark their discipline.

> I thought statistics could rescue something from all the math that I had learned and that led me into statistical studies. Today, I think it probably was a good thing that I was able to combine my scientific mind with my love for mathematics and history. Mathematics gave me an ability to make connections. I do well in making connections between different ideas, almost like a physical structure. That is what mathematics does, making connections and help organize your thinking. (Fig. 2.4)

During the war, the Right was nonexistent at LSE and this reflected the diversity of the left at the time. The Anarchists were considered the most radical, followed by Communist militants, then Socialists, and trade unionists. This was a historical anomaly since LSE was conservative and close to the upper echelons of London's financial district. The war effort monopolized the time of established British economists. Kari Polanyi took pleasure at LSE, where leftist ideas dominating echoed those of Red Vienna.

Fig. 2.4 Kari at LSE, 1941–42

> The student movement in England was dominated by the Communist party. Because of the rise of Hitler and the Spanish civil war, many bright young people thought that the Soviet Union was the only way to defeat fascism. While I was at the LSE, communists were at the center and had the brightest of the students. On the left, there were pacifists and on the right was the Labour Party. Beyond the Labour Party, there was nothing. There were no conservatives, no liberals.

Studying in wartime had benefits. Due to the London bombings, the London campus was evacuated and relocated to Cambridge, where LSE students had access to courses from both schools. This enabled students to benefit from the courses offered by a multitude of eminent economists, such as Joan Robinson and Sir Arthur Lewis. Nicholas Kaldor's course was of particular interest as he dealt with the history of economic thought by analyzing each of its milestones, from Smith to Marx.

After the war, Kari Polanyi got involved in a research project led by Kaldor on the effects of allied bombings on the German economy

(*British Bombing Survey Unit*, 1945–1947; Kaldor 1945).[2] She spoke of Kaldor with great admiration. Initially a disciple of Hayek and part of the neoclassical school of economics, he became an influential thinker of the Keynesian school.

> "My favorite, from whom I have learned so much and remembered all through my career in economics, was Kaldor. His course on Economic Analysis was presented as a history of economic thought. He presented Adam Smith and the exchange of beavers and dears, that old story. He proceeded to deconstruct his thought; likewise with Ricardo, and then on with Marx and the marginalist revolution. I will never forget how the course ended. "*Ladies and gentlemen, there is currently a research survey to find out how businessmen set their prices. They report that they sum up the costs and they add a margin; so, you see we still do not know the source of value.*" I attended a course with F. von Hayek. He lectured chapter by chapter using a large textbook written by Kenneth Boulding that my father called "The Boulder". After a few weeks, students stopped attending as you could just read the book. We were never exposed to Hayek's theories and ideas."

Kari Polanyi was at the forefront when the first debates surrounding the problem of underdevelopment in large parts of the world economy appeared. Kaldor, like Arthur Lewis, Raúl Prebisch,[3] and Celso Furtado,

[2] Nicholas Kaldor (1908–1986) was a British Economist born in Budapest. Considered one of the main authors of the post-Keynesian movement, he advised British Labour governments (1964–1968, 1974–1976) as well as governments of developing countries. His most influential works are those dealing with economic cycles. Kaldor innovated by considering the nonlinearity of the relationship between savings and investment. The propensity to save is transformed at the peaks of the cycle: In the lows, investors will be more cautious, because the spillovers are less important, and in the highs, the rise in costs discourages investments. Kaldor attached great importance to the distribution of income, arguing that the rich and the poor have different savings practices, the latter being more inclined to save when conditions are favorable. Because of the different savings behaviors between workers and capital owners, savings will continue to increase, which will weaken the cycle. In times of depression, prices must fall faster than wages, which will reduce savings to the benefit of consumption, stifling the depressive cycle.

[3] Raúl Prebisch (1901–1986), an Argentine Economist, was recognized for his important contribution to the foundations of the dependency theory. In 1948, he became director of the Economic Commission for Latin America and the Caribbean (ECLAC), a position which he held until 1963. Under his leadership, ECLAC became the main engine of Third-World activism. He founded the Latin American school. Rather than waiting for aid from developed countries, Prebisch recommended that developing countries carry out

was looking into the question of development economics in the 1940s and 1950s with the support of the United Nations. Economic development became one of the main subjects in Kari Polanyi's work.

> Prebisch created the Latin American structuralist economic doctrine or school and gave it an institutional base at the ECLAC at the United Nations. After he retired from UN, notably as president of UNCTAD, he worked for the *Alliance for Progress* and became disillusioned about international agencies. Like Myrdal, he believed that there was not much to be gained from international negotiations. Myrdal was a gigantic figure because he was an important economist in the development of the Swedish model. He was the first Secretary General of the European Commission in the United Nations and was originally a supporter of international assistance. Later in his life, he denounced the international aid industry.

LSE curriculum did not include fundamental authors. The theories of John Maynard Keynes were not studies, although their influence was increasing. Polanyi became acquainted with Keynes' ideas through her proximity to Kaldor and Kalecki.

> Thanks to Kaldor, I knew the basics of the Keynesian approach that was not taught in my courses. We were aware of Keynes' proposal of 1942 issued as an official government white paper, a blueprint for a new post-war international financial order. It was widely discussed but LSE was not friendly to Keynes as Lionel Robbins had brought Hayek from Vienna in 1931 for the specific purpose of combating the dangerous influence of Keynes they believed to be inflationary. LSE was close to the *City*. Keynes was feared because people in the City thought that deficit financing would create inflation. When I wrote my final exam in 1947, Keynes was not on the curriculum. At Cambridge, there were off campus classes in Keynesian economics taught by young LSE lecturers. Interestingly, we were

domestic reforms. He developed the theory of the declining terms of trade, which will become the basis of Dependency theory. See: Prebisch, 1950 and 1959. His approach is centered on trade, more particularly on the preferential access of developing countries to international trade. From 1964 to 1969, he was the first Secretary-General of the United Nations Conference on Trade and Development (UNCTAD). During his years at ECLA, Prebisch promoted a strategy of industrialization through import-substitution. This doctrine advocated a temporary isolation of international trade in order to use the internal and regional market to industrialize. Several years later, while at UNCTAD, Prebisch distanced himself from this doctrine, recognizing that it had not produced the expected results.

discovering Kalecki and Marx in classes offered by the Communist Party off campus.

According to Kari Polanyi, Kalecki's contribution to economics was underestimated as he predicted that full employment targeted by Keynes would have the unfortunate consequence of causing predatory behavior on the part of the capitalist classes. Kalecki thought Keynesian policies would lead to the emergence of neoliberalism, which Kari Polanyi called the "neoliberal counter-revolution."

> Kalecki was prescient in his prediction that the Keynesian solution would ultimately fail. He argued that full employment for a long period of time, as in 1950s and 60s, the power of the capitalist class would weaken to such a degree that they would find it intolerable. The neoliberal counter-revolution was constructed in think tanks as a response to the concern of the capitalist class that the world was getting out of control, both domestically and internationally.

First Steps in the World of Work

During her studies in England, Kari Polanyi worked in a factory during the holidays, creating her links with the working world. In 1943, when the war was raging, she wanted to get involved in the women's division of the armed forces, it was no longer recruiting. She chose to return to the working world as her summer work experiences helped her to create an important network. She joined a major union of war industry workers, the *Amalgamated Engineering Union*. She was invited to work for the research department composed of three women. This research department remained in London during the war, while the vast majority of its administrators relocated outside the capital to flee the bombardments. These years would mark her deeply. She pursued her interest in unionism and in the social dynamics of capitalism.

> After the first two years at the LSE, I was called up for National Service. I was told that I could find my own employment. My ambition was to specialize in labour research. I had done some voluntary work with the labour research department built by a wonderful woman by the name of Margot Heinemann and I found employment in the research department of the *Amalgamated Engineering Union*, representing over a million workers employed in the war industries. During the war, the research

department was located in South London and it was entirely staffed by women. The director was Yvonne Kaap[4] who had previously worked at Vogue in Paris.

After the war, she resumed her studies at LSE to complete the two remaining years required to obtain her undergraduate degree in economics with a specialization in statistics. She was very successful and actually tied for the first spot with Ralph Turvey, but Maurice Dobb broke the tie in Turvey's favor. She had fellowship offers from LSE and she also worked with the famous team led by Kaldor on *The Effects of Allied Strategic Bombing on the German War Economy*. Had she stayed in Europe, she stated that she would have probably gone to Geneva to work with Gunnar Myrdal at the United Nations.

> Kaldor invited me to join his team on the famous British study on *The Effects of Allied Strategic Bombing on the German War Economy*. There was a small team in Britain led by Kaldor and a very large American team led by John Kenneth Galbraith. This is how Kaldor and Galbraith met. When the British and the American forces invaded Germany, they seized documents on war production from the German war factories and brought them to London and to Washington to be analyzed. The British team consisted of Kaldor, who directed it, a professional statistician and myself. I was hired because I could read German and my task was to look at microfiches and record the information. The study found that the result of the heavy bombing of German industrial cities and the working class population was a constant increase of production. You can demolish structures but you can't demolish the will of a people. The German bombings had a similar effect in England.

Kari Polanyi, following the footsteps of her mother, joined the Communist Party and became friends with a group of Canadians who came to London on a voluntary basis to combat the rise of fascism in

[4] Yvonne Kapp (1903–1999) was a very influential and creative person. She published a masterpiece biography of 1000 pages on Eleanor Marx (Kapp 1977; Hobsbawm 1999).

Europe. She met Joseph Levitt,[5] a Canadian soldier also a member of the Communist Party.

> I had met in England Canadians who had volunteered to fight fascism, including Joe Levitt, and I agreed to join him in Canada when I finished my studies. He was demobilized in 1946 and I came to Canada in 1947. I thought Canada would resemble Britain, allowing you to engage in any political activity of your choice, including the Communist Party. I discovered that although that was the case in theory, in fact it was quite different.

References

Clancier, Philippe, Francis Joannès, Pierre Rouillard and Aline Tenu. 2005. *Autour de Polanyi: Vocabulaires, théories et modalités des échanges*. Paris: De Boccard.

Dale, Gareth. 2010. *Karl Polanyi: The Limits of The Market*. Cambridge: Polity Press.

Dale, Gareth. 2015. *Karl Polanyi: The Hungarian Writings*. Manchester: Manchester University Press.

Dale, Gareth. 2016. *Karl Polanyi; A Life on the Left*. New York: Columbia University Press.

Hobsbawm, Eric. 1999. *Industry and Empire: From 1750 to the Present Day*. New York: The New Press.

Kaldor, Nicholas. 1945. 'The German War Economy.' *The Review of Economic Studies* 13: 33–52.

Kapp, Yvonne. 1977. *Eleanor Marx*. New York: Pantheon Books.

Maucourant, Jérôme. 2011. *Avez-vous lu Polanyi?* Paris: Flammarion.

[5] Joe Levitt, Montrealer of origin, whose family had moved to the Toronto area in the 1930s, had decided to put aside his studies and enlisted in the Canadian Army to help fight the rise of fascism in Europe. He served in many positions, both in France, Belgium, Germany, and Italy, during the war and was decorated for the courage and leadership he demonstrated during a battle in Normandy. Returning to Toronto, he resumed his studies and obtained a doctorate in history. He became a professor at the University of Ottawa and is recognized as a specialist of a Quebec politician Henri Bourassa. Kari Polanyi and Joe Levitt married in 1950 in Toronto and had two children, Tom and Harry. Joe Levitt died in 2009. See Joseph Levitt. *Henri Bourassa and the Golden Calf: The Social Program of the Nationalists of Quebec (1900–1914)*. (Cahiers d'histoire, Number 3). Ottawa: Éditions de l'Université d'Ottawa. 1969. Pp. ix, 178.

Maucourant, Jérôme and Sébastien Plociniczak. 2011. 'Penser l'institution et le marché avec Karl Polanyi; Contre la crise (de la pensée) économique.' *Revue de la régulation* 10. Accessed April 21, 2021. http://regulation.revues.org/9439

McRobbie, Kenneth and Kari Polanyi-Levitt (eds.). 2000. *Karl Polanyi in Vienna: The Contemporary Significance of the Great Transformation*, 346. Montreal, Canada: Black Rose Books.

Polanyi Levitt, Kari. 1990a. *The Life and Work of Karl Polanyi*. Montreal: Black Rose Books.

Polanyi Levitt, Kari. 1990b. Debt, Adjustment and Development: Looking to the 1990s. *Economic and Political Weekly* 25: 1585–1594.

CHAPTER 3

Trajectory of Life, Part 2: Crossing the Ocean to Canada and the Caribbean

Abstract This chapter recounts the main landmarks in Kari Polanyi Levitt's career: She publishes her main success *Silent Surrender*, documenting the domination of the Canadian economy by multinationals. Along with Kaldor, Arthur Lewis, Raúl Prebisch, and Celso Furtado, she is at the forefront when the first debates surrounding the problem of global underdevelopment appeared. She further develops her thoughts on economic dependence while in the Caribbean, playing a major role in the design of the Plantation Economy Model, which highlights dependence patterns unique to the region.

Keywords Development studies · Economic dependency · Multinational corporations (MNCs) · Plantation economy model · Silent surrender

The landing in Toronto in 1947 was difficult for Kari Polanyi Levitt. After Vienna and London, Toronto seems dull. It was the first time that she was in a former colony, and she realized that Toronto, although one of the biggest cities in Canada, was in the periphery of the world economy (Figs. 3.1, 3.2, 3.3, 3.4, 3.5, 3.6 and 3.7).

Joe Levitt had contacted the University of Toronto where Kari Polanyi Levitt was planning to pursue graduate studies. This is how she was introduced to Harold Innis. She was happy to reunite with her parents. In the

M. Rioux and H. Brisson, *Kari Polanyi Levitt and Canadian Political Economy*, https://doi.org/10.1007/978-3-030-87364-6_3

Fig. 3.1 Kari—Editor of the Mine & Mill Herald—Toronto (mid 1950s)

Fig. 3.2 Kari—Electoral campaign and Editor Mine & Mill Herald—Toronto

Fig. 3.3 Kari 1952—With son Tom and Karl Polanyi

Fig. 3.4 1949, Labour Day Toronto

late 1940s, Karl Polanyi had been invited to teach at Columbia University in New York City. But in the middle of McCarthyism, it was impossible for Ilona, an active member of the Communist Party, to follow her husband to the United States. They had a residence in Pickering, Ontario, and Karl was traveling between the two cities. Their house in Pickering became a meeting place for several renowned intellectuals and students, including Marshall McLuhan. Kari Polanyi Levitt enjoyed this climate, similar to what she had experienced in London and Vienna.

Fig. 3.5 Kari, Joe Levitt with friend (New York, 1947)

> Joe had [...] very thoughtfully made contact with the university of Toronto, thinking that I would continue graduate studies. I spent the first year at the University of Toronto. I had a teaching assistantship in a course on economic history, a subject that I knew very well [...] I enjoyed that but I found the atmosphere oppressive and I decided I wanted to pursue my interest in the labour movement and labour research.

Hired as a machinist at the *Acme Screw and Gear Company*, a manufacturer of parts for automobiles and war equipment, she became involved in the *Union of Automobile Workers* that later became the *Canadian Automobile Workers*. She devoted a large part of her time to write in the union's newspaper. A few years later, the *United Electrical Workers* asked her to be part of their research team. She later moved on to work for the *Union of Mine, Mill, and Smelter Workers*. From 1948 to 1956, she devoted the first eight years of her life in Canada to the world of work. She has great memories of those years of integration into Canadian society, during which she forged lasting friendships.

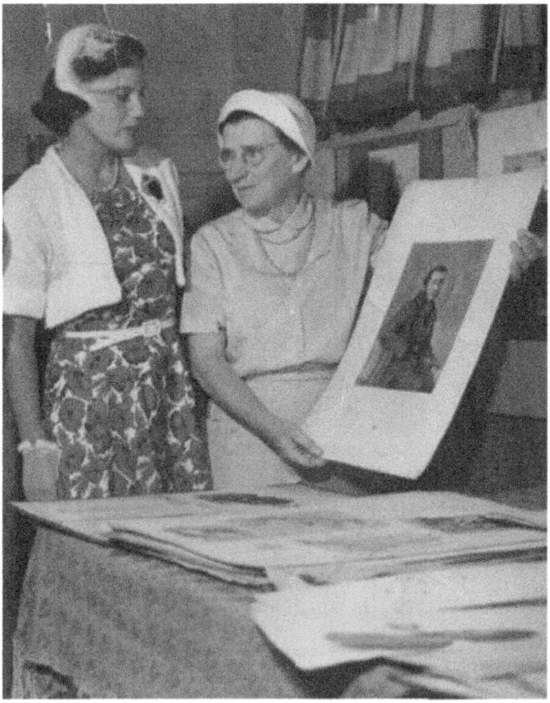

Fig. 3.6 Kari with her mother Ilona Duczynska (donation of artworks to Poland, belonging to Ilona's family, dating back to the nineteenth century)

Following the Soviet repression of the Budapest uprising, many members of the Communist Party from Europe and America severed ties with the political party linked to the USSR. Former sympathizers dissociated themselves from a regime which has flouted the socialist ideals of peace and freedom. Kari Polanyi Levitt teared up her membership card of the Party and questioned her engagement in the social movements, which had been an important part of her identity.

> In 1956, like many others, I resigned from the Communist Party after the Hungarian revolution and the invasion by the Soviet Union. It seemed that I had wasted many years. I needed to get back to my studies and considered a change. Information technology was beginning, and opportunities were offered to students with an undergraduate degree. I decided to enroll

Fig. 3.7 1957—Kari and Karl (Ontario)

in a master's program in Economics at the University of Toronto. I did two years of the program and every courses required by the PhD program.

Back to Graduate Studies: Passion for Development Studies and Early Recruitment by McGill University

Kari Polanyi Levitt rediscovered the interest she had in Kaldor's teachings and deepened her knowledge of Canadian economic history, especially through the work of Harold Innis. She was taking Stephen Triantis's course on economic development and conducted research on the factors explaining the underdevelopment.

She undertook doctoral studies, but McGill University offered her a full-time professor position in Economics before she could complete the program. McGill University offered her to teach a course in economic planning, an area in which she had an expertise but she also had to teach subjects in which she was not specialized. She considered that teaching different courses allowed the broadening of her knowledge of new areas of economic discipline.

> I was teaching a very heavy load. They gave me a course on economic planning. I was given a course about which I knew nothing, banking. I taught a course on business cycles, which I found interesting but the problem was that in the sixties, business cycles had disappeared, and the course morphed into a course on economic growth. In the case of the banking course, I would start at five o'clock in the morning to have time to read the next chapter in the textbook and I would present myself at 9 o'clock totally familiar with the material. I was strict with the students because I knew that this was a contest between my authority, as a relatively young woman, and a large class of students, mostly male. If I did not exert my authority, I would be in trouble.

Kari Polanyi Levitt had agreed to participate in a research on inputs and outputs of the Canadian Maritime provinces' economy, which was, at that time, economically underdeveloped when compared to the rest of the country. For this project, Kari Polanyi Levitt collaborated with Statistics Canada and its staff, which included several graduates from McGill University.

> "In 1961, I received a job offer from McGill, which was at the prompting of professor Keirstead. I started at McGill without finishing the PhD and I had to produce an input–output analysis for the Maritimes. I got engaged to conduct the input–output study of the Atlantic Provinces". I has been introduced to national accounting at LSE through a book written by J. R. Hicks, *The social framework: An Introduction to Economics* (1952), that presented the system of national accounts in terms of major sectors.

The data collected in the Maritime Provinces was used to determine whether it was better to encourage industries to settle in the region or whether to encourage local populations to emigrate to more prosperous regions. Kari Polanyi Levitt advocated the first solution. She was convinced that it was better to provide aid for the promotion of development of the region. This project was the stepping stone of her intellectual journey as it became a source of a multidisciplinary research that she would later undertake with Lloyd Best in the Caribbean that would later lead to the theory of Plantation Economy model (Polanyi Levitt 2005a).

In the 1970s, economists were increasingly turning their attention to development studies. Discovering the contributions of economists Celso Furtado[1] and Osvaldo Sunkel, Kari Polanyi Levitt noted that she agreed with many of their ideas. In 1970, Sunkel,[2] whom she had first met in the mid-1960s, decided to bring together several economists to Hamburg to discuss the problem of economic dependency. Among them Polanyi Levitt, Lloyd Best, Mel Watkins, Giovanni Arrighi, and Stephen Hymer. They became close collaborators of Kari Polanyi Levitt as well as important authors in "the sociology of development" or development studies. Using different paths, they arrived at similar conclusions. Polanyi Levitt told us in an interview that it was during this meeting that she realized she belonged to that intellectual circle.

> Osvaldo Sunkel's meeting was important because it brought together people from different places working independently who nevertheless were looking at the world in a similar way. There was a great excitement for people who had independently done work to compare their insights. Arrighi once said to me: "You know, Kari, if you put together the insights of your father and my geometry of imperialism..." it would resonate. I couldn't understand! But it became clear to me that my father's first pages of *The Great Transformation* talked about four institutions that define the

[1] Celso Furtado (1920–2004) was a Brazilian Economist. His best-known work, *The Economic Growth of Brazil* (1963), on the economic history of Brazil and the causes of its underdevelopment, is considered a classic. He saw underdevelopment as a structural process inherent to capitalism, which contradicts the dominant idea of the time, according to which underdevelopment is a stage leading toward development. This situation could not be corrected without strong state intervention to redirect the surpluses of the upper classes to productive sectors rather than to the consumption of imported luxury consumer goods.

[2] Osvaldo Sunkel is a Chilean economist. His work focused on the mining sector, inflation, development, socio-economic history, international relations, and regional integration. His best-known work is *El Subdesarrollo Latinoamericano y la Teoría del Desarrollo*, co-written with Pedro Paz (Sunkel and Paz 1970). He came to Montreal in 2003 and 2004 at the invitation of CEIM to participate in international conferences on integration in the Americas and inequalities.

world capitalist system from 1870 to 1914 or 1930 and that he was missing a fifth institution, political colonialism, an institution of the nineteenth century international world order.

The resurgence of liberal ideas in the 1970s, what Kari Polanyi Levitt called a *neoliberal counter—revolution*, led to a declining interest in Keynesian economics. The new multidisciplinary approach, the sociology or political economy of development, was relegated to marginality.

Kari Polanyi Levitt continued to be interested in the question of development and sought to contribute to the criticism of neoliberal ideas highlighting the abuses that capitalism without proper institutional regulation can engender. She produced two main great contributions, the book *Silent Surrender* (Polanyi Levitt 2003b) and the development of the *Plantation economy model* (Polanyi Levitt and Best 2009).

Silent Surrender: Canada as a Developed Dependent Country

In the late 1960s, Kari Polanyi Levitt analyzed the issue of foreign investment in Canada. Her first contribution on the subject was published in the *New World Quarterly* under the title "*Economic Dependence and Political Disintegration: The Case of Canada*" (Polanyi Levitt 1968). This article and the work behind it would then grow into what would become her flagship work—*Silent Surrender* (Polanyi Levitt 2003b), first published in 1970.[3]

At the time, the literature on multinational corporations (MNCs) was scarce. Kari Polanyi Levitt was connected with Charles Kindleberger, Stephen Hymer, Raymond Vernon, and Harold Innis, who were among the leading scholars working on foreign direct investment.

> My insights came from many people. I had that idea before reading the authors, but things resonated with Charles Kindleberger, Mira Wilkins and Raymond Vernon. Harold Innis wrote on the fur trade and that made a big impression on me. I remember thinking about mixing his ideas with Vernon's concept of product cycle and Schumpeter's ideas about innovation and competition. Stephen Hymer was obviously a great influence for

[3] Kari Polanyi Levitt, 'Economic Dependence and Political Disintegration, The Case of Canada,' *New World Quarterly* 4 (2), 1968.

> me. We would often talk until three in the morning! One summer, he was leaving as the sun was coming up, and I remember him saying goodbye. It was the last time I saw him before he had a car accident that tragically killed him.

At that time, the Canadian political elite largely subscribed to the idea that foreign investments generated profits. The NDP wanted to develop its position on foreign investment and the ever-growing presence of American multinational companies in Canada. Charles Taylor, a reknown McGill professor, suggested that Kari Polanyi Levitt authored a report to advise the NDP (Rioux and Brisson 2012). Kari Polanyi Levitt was invited to the NDP's executive committee meeting, chaired by David Lewis, to discuss her research.

Kari Polanyi Levitt was convinced that the loss of control of Canadian industries falling in the hands of foreign interests—mainly American—posed a threat to Canadian sovereignty. Therefore, she advised the NDP to adopt a strong stance against foreign investments. But the NDP was afraid that questioning foreign investment would hurt Canadian workers. In certain key sectors, notably the automobile industry, thousands of Canadian workers worked in a cross-border environment because of the importance of North American economic integration. The NDP chose to put aside Polanyi Levitt's recommendations. However, this was not the end of it since the article was published in a Caribbean journal (Polanyi Levitt 1968) and copies of the article circulated in academic circles across Canada.

> "Colleagues in the West Indies had a journal called *New World Quarterly*. Lloyd Best, a colleague from Trinidad, told me "this is wonderful, we are going to publish your article in the *New World Quarterly*." It was published as "*Economic Dependence and Political Disintegration, The Case of Canada.*" What happened was amazing because this obscure Caribbean journal began to circulate in Canada. Cy Gonick, editor of a left-wing journal, put it between two covers and launched it as a special publication with wide circulation particularly in student circles. The idea of a book emerged".

Cy Gonick, chief editor of the left-wing publication *Canadian Dimension,* published it in the form of a leaflet.

Her colleague, Professor Eric Kierans, helped her gather data to broaden her research. She found an attractive title—*Silent Surrender:*

Multinational Corporations in Canada—that was proposed, in fact, by one of her sons. She submitted the manuscript to Macmillan of Canada. The editor, very keen on publishing it, asked Polanyi Levitt to suggest an evaluator. The book was sent to Mel Watkins, who even offered to write a Preface. *Silent Surrender—The American Economic Empire in Canada* appeared in 1971.

The impact of this book was significant, as its reedition and reimpressions can attest. It was widely talked about and was mentioned in the economic section of the Saturday edition of the *New York Times*. Polanyi Levitt's book found her audience in the nationalist circles of Quebec, Canada, and abroad. It met with favorable reception in independentist circles in Quebec where it was published in French in 2002 under the title *La capitulation tranquille* with a preface written by the eminent economist, who became a Premier of Quebec, Jacques Parizeau (*Parti Québécois*) (Watkins 2005, 106).

"I expanded the original article, and together with my son Tom we came up with an appealing title: *Silent Surrender*. I approached Macmillan. It was sent to a reader, an economist, who rejected the manuscript as "unprofessional and unacceptable." But the editor who had worked on the manuscript believed that it should be published. She asked me if I could suggest another reader. I proposed Mel Watkins. The rest is history. Mel was very enthusiastic. It was reprinted many times and sold 40,000 copies, and even earned an unexpected and considerable sum in royalties. It was translated into French as *La Capitulation tranquille*, with an introduction by Jacques Parizeau, then a professor at the HEC."

Following the Watkins' report (Ottawa Privy Council Office 1968),[4] *Silent Surrender* made the most radical analysis of foreign investment in Canada. The book described Canada as a country with significant wealth and industrialized status, but whose economy is structured like that of an underdeveloped country. Like the Watkins report, *Silent Surrender* dealt with the threat that multinationals pose to the sovereignty of nations (Watkins 2005).

Silent Surrender analyzed foreign direct investments in Canada. According to Polanyi Levitt, a subsidiary of a MNC established in Canada responds to strategies of its parent company, and therefore, Canada will

[4] Mel Watkins Report is Ottawa privy council.

have difficulty putting effective policies for long-term industrial development. Polanyi Levitt showed that subsidiaries of MNCs cannot have either their own resources in research and development or decision-making authority allowing for the development and the coordination of a national industrialization strategy. As a result, since the majority of companies are not under Canadian control, Canada is confined to a status of a raw material exporting country even if it wanted to develop other economic sectors. She associated this phenomenon with the loss of state sovereignty over the national territory. Today, the threat of losing sovereignty is represented by the weight of Big Tech interests.

Silent Surrender innovated by questioning the economic policies of Canada based on the first and most influential research on MNCs as economic actors. With the strong presence of American MNCs in Canada, the Canadian economy was "silently" in the process of becoming subordinated to US capitalism and politics. At that time, the manufacturing sector was the heart of the Canadian economy, notably the automobile sector. When the most dynamic sector of the economy is controlled by foreign interests, the host country is in a trajectory leading to a gradual loss of control of its economy.

In her book, Kari Polanyi Levitt distanced herself from the Marxist approach anchored in determinism, neglecting actors and the impacts they can have on the system. Combining Marxist and Schumpeterian approaches, she retained the ontology of the first and blended it with Schumpeter's emphasis on innovation. This was an interesting way to offset the shortcoming of traditional Marxist theories linking profits exclusively to labor and to introduce innovation in the equation.

For Kari, the Canadian economy, like those of Third World countries, was economically dependent on the export of raw materials and natural resources. Canada had the characteristics of a neocolonial economic model and was the developed country that was the most "dependent" in the world economy. According to her, the development of a national economy is linked to entrepreneurship and innovations. In a situation of dependency, innovation is held back, while it is stimulated in the center economies. She predicted the decline of the Canadian economy because US interests increasingly controlled key economic sectors, while making calls to curb or, at least, to control this trend. The book was one of the first criticisms of the rise of US MNCs in Canada. It analyzed the early signs of capitalist globalization, and more importantly, it predicted the high social cost of this phenomenon. Canada decided to adopt the

Foreign Investment Review Act to control foreign investment but it was abandoned in the 1980s to be replaced by the *Investment Act* aimed at attracting foreign investment on more liberal grounds.

McGill University did not agree with the importance of Silent Surrender. The committee to decide her promotion for full professor were extremely critical. When they asked her how she viewed *Silent Surrender*, she answered: "I think it is the most important thing that I have ever done, maybe the most important thing that I will do for the rest of my career." They looked stunned as the book received negative reviews. They insisted that she would get her full professorship once she would finish her research on the Maritime Provinces. They could not understand how someone with her competence and mathematical skills could write something with so little substance. Kari Polanyi Levitt rarely submitted articles to peer-reviewed journals and was never motivated to do that. She understands that she was fortunate to enjoy the privilege and liberty to choose what she considered important to publish. It would certainly be impossible nowadays to become a full professor in a university like McGill without having a PhD and published in scientific journals.

Kari Polanyi Levitt believed in the intervention of the state to regulate the economy to ensure social and economic development. This is also expressed in her scientific contributions to the development of the Plantation Economy Model.

Caribbean Life: The Emergence of the Plantation Economy Model

When Kari Polanyi Levitt established herself in Montreal, she also made her first contact with the Caribbean where she was involved in a multitude of activities. Among her many activities were teaching, researching, and participating in conferences, taking part in public debates, organizing student exchanges, and acting as a consultant. Even recently, she returned to visit friends and attend conferences. She was able to discover the Caribbean countries when they were in a pivotal period in their history as a wind of change was blowing over the region as a result of the pressure of a strong anti-colonialist and pan-Caribbean movement. Most countries in the region had just gained independence and a revolutionary government had been established in Cuba (Fig. 3.8).

In the late 1950s and early 1960s, studies were launched in the region to prepare for the ambitious plan to create a Confederation of Caribbean

Fig. 3.8 Kari in Trinidad

states. In December 1960, Professor B. S. Keirstead invited Kari Polanyi Levitt to participate in a research project aiming to integrate shipping and transport services between Caribbean islands. The two weeks she spent in Jamaica left a strong impression on her.

> My contact with the Caribbean came shortly before I accepted the position at McGill in 1961. It was the time of the Federation of the West Indies, which collapsed in 1962. Keirstead had a sabbatical leave and was invited by Arthur Lewis to undertake a study on the federal shipping service. Keirstead called me and when I visited the region Ifelt I had stepped back into the nineteenth century, the world of the novels of Jane Austen. It

was very colonial. I was sent to Trinidad where I met a number of young economists who had been trained in Britain at the LSE or at Cambridge, with whom I had much in common.

In the spring of 1961, she was invited to return to the Caribbean. It was during these first two stays that Polanyi Levitt met intellectuals from the region, such as Lloyd Best, Williams Demas, Alister McIntyre, and George Beckford, with whom she forged professional links and friendships. She integrated into the effervescent atmosphere instilled by decolonization. She joined the New World Group movement, which Lloyd Best created with other intellectuals from Guyana, and participated in the launch of a publication, the *New World Quarterly*, in which the article that led to *Silent Surrender* was first published.

She deepened her ties with Lloyd Best.[5] Together, they characterized the economic history of the Caribbean through a model called the Plantation Economy. The model considered the appropriation of local labor by landowners, i.e., slavery, as a form of capital. The workforce made up of African slaves participated in a form of division of labor on a world scale. This model was a departure from the ideas of an influential scholar from Saint Lucia, Arthur Lewis.

Although Lewis[6] was successful in applying a classical Ricardian analysis, yet, he thereby omitted various important internal and social factors specific to the Caribbean Islands. Lloyd Best and Kari Polanyi Levitt departed from the point of view that the theory of Ricardo was applicable

[5] Lloyd Best (1934–2007) was an Economist from Trinidad. He was Professor of Economics at the University of the West Indies and Leader of the Opposition in the Senate of Trinidad and Tobago. He was the Founder of the Trinidad and Tobago Institute of the West Indies which will be renamed the Lloyd Best Institute of the West Indies in his honor after his death in 2007. Lloyd Best is one of the founders of the New World Group (NWG) founded in 1962 in Guyana. This group brought together various intellectuals from the Caribbean to develop a theory that would explain the economic and societal dynamics of the countries of the region.

[6] Arthur Lewis was one of the most influential Caribbean intellectuals. As Ghana gained independence, he was appointed head of the national development plan. In recognition of his contributions to the economy, Lewis was knighted by the Queen of England in 1963 and awarded the Nobel Prize in economics in 1979 for his work on development. His work put unemployment at the core of the difficulties of Caribbean countries to reach a continuous level of development. He advocated for the massive arrival of foreign companies in the region to create jobs. But the approach of Polanyi Levitt and Best highlighted new systemic causes to explain the economic stagnation of the Caribbean countries.

to Caribbean countries, because they participated in the international division of labor with strong specialization and were, almost exclusively, oriented toward exports. Such a situation was completely detached from the traditional local spheres of political or cultural control, and thus, the Ricardian model was irrelevant.[7]

Polanyi Levitt and Best incorporated into their model the fact that those societies were made up mainly of populations brought from different regions of the world, a historic characteristic almost unique to the Caribbean. These different groups constituted heavily segmented social strata, which complicated the formation of a common identity and undermined the potential for political mobilization. They integrated notions of economic sociology into their approach; they considered the general absence of a long-term vision, among operators and workers, as a factor curbing the emergence and functioning of a local market capable of promoting development. In such a system, the financial sphere is organized to facilitate the outflow of capital to send to the metropole. This capital flight prevented the construction of a local economy independent from the metropole.

There were three phases identified in their mode (Polanyi Levitt and Best 2009).

- The first historical phase (1600–1838) was characterized by slavery as a mode of production.
- The second phase (1839–1938) was marked by the abolition of slavery and the introduction of wages for the workers.

[7] With Adam Smith and James Mill, David Ricardo (1772–1823) was regarded as one of the most important British economists of Classic liberal economic thought (Ricardo 2001 (1817]). His most important work focused on value theory, rent and land theory, the gold standard and comparative advantage. Ricardo's essential contribution lies mainly in his theory of comparative advantages. According to this theory, all countries find it beneficial to specialize in the production of a good for which they have the greatest relative advantage or the least significant disadvantage. Four conditions must be met however: The value of labor is equivalent to the price multiplied by the quantity of labor, competition is perfect, only goods circulate internationally and not the factors of production, and finally, productivity is constant. The country specializing in the export of specific products is forced to import products which it no longer produces because of its specialization. This idea was heavily criticized in debates concerning countries' dependency on international trade.

- The third phase was distinguished by the emergence of a diversification of the economic activities which were in competition with those of the agriculture sector.

The role of multinational corporations was at the center of their approach. This historical perspective showed how much MNCs had intervened in the consolidation of hierarchical relations in the region by organizing their activities depending on the branch and the location. The model of the plantation economy drew attention to another unique historical feature of multinationals' activities in the region: They are mainly concentrated on the extraction of raw materials or commodities, mainly sugar. MNCs operating in the center of the world economy are more generally active in manufacturing or services (Best 2005).

Lloyd Best and Kari Polanyi Levitt drew from several structuralist economists in Latin America. Polanyi Levitt cited the important work *The Economic Growth of Brazil* by Celso Furtado (1963) or contributions of Dudley Seers, Samir Amin, and Oswaldo Sunkel who developed the dependency theory. Seers, who worked in Venezuela on ECLA projects, created the *Institute of Development Studies* in 1963 at the University of Sussex. When visiting at the University of Sussex, Kari Polanyi Levitt met Sunkel, who later became a friend.

> "Chilean of German descent, Sunkel spoke beautiful high German. He wrote a number of articles about dependency, but I knew only the ones in English. One was very similar to a paper I had written in 1968 about structures of dependency. In 1970, Osvaldo organized a conference in Hamburg sponsored by the Max Planck Institute gathering authors from Canada, Mel Watkins and me, from the Caribbean, Lloyd Best, and he invited Giovanni Arrighi from East Africa. He also invited Stephen Hymer. It was small, more like a "working weekend" rather than a conference. I remember the excitement of people from different places who, independently, had got a rather similar perception of the world system."

The Plantation Economy Model filled a theoretical void by considering the peculiarities of the Caribbean colonial heritage. Best asserted that Polanyi Levitt's work in the region helped reverse the Caribbean colonial dynamic (Best 2008). The theory of plantation economics offered an innovative approach to the intersection of class and race relationships, which continues to be a relevant tool to understand the domination of certain classes that still prevails in certain countries of the region (Girvan 2005).

Although the model of the plantation economy was developed in the 1960s, it was not until 2009 that a work about it was first published (Polanyi Levitt and Best 2009). Despite this late publication, the model was known in academic and intellectual circles in the region, thanks to lectures, unofficial texts, and the teaching activities of Polanyi Levitt and Best at the University of the West Indies. It influenced three generations of Caribbean researchers from different disciplines. Even today, this approach is embraced by several researchers in the region, to the point that the designation "Plantation School" refers to a Caribbean school in social sciences.[8]

The model allowed Caribbean researchers and intellectuals to explain the dynamics and the historical trajectory of the region without resorting to imported models. The concern for historicity meant that economic policies could not be considered independent from the historical context of the society in which they are elaborated. Thus, the model is critical of international institutions and governments that want to adopt a one-size-fits-all development model, constituting one of its main legacies.

Following her first trips to the region, she and her family spent a few years in the region. In 1969, Lloyd Best invited her to settle in Trinidad and Tobago to join the university research group he led at the *Institute of Social and Economic Research* for a project funded by the Canadian International Development Agency (CIDA). However, it was short-lived as the donor withdrew the funds. Kari Polanyi Levitt and her family stayed in Trinidad and Tobago, thanks to William Demas, an economist at the head of the *Caribbean Development Bank,* who invited her to participate in the setting up of a national statistics system as part of a new national planning strategy (Polanyi Levitt 2005a). The work done for this project (1969–1973) was impressive, particularly from a methodological and statistical point of view as everything had to be built from scratch.

To extend her Caribbean experience, she accepted a three-year position as a visiting professor at the *Institute of International Relations* on the Jamaican campus of the University of the West Indies. This professional

[8] Lloyd Best thought this designation was reductive (Best 2008), because many have adopted this theoretical approach to address widely diverse subjects, far exceeding the study of a colonial economic system built around plantation operations.

adventure ended abruptly when her work permit was revoked (Polanyi Levitt 2005a).

> With Lloyd Best, I had a grant from McGill from the *Center for Developing Areas Studies* to develop our Plantation Economy Model for the Caribbean. I had planned to move for two years with the family to Trinidad. I accepted an invitation from Mr. William Demas, chief economist for Trinidad, to produce a new database for the next five-year plan for the country, a project financed by IMF Technical Assistance and strongly supported by the government of Trinidad and Tobago. Basically, I was an adviser on the new system of national economic accounts.

The task was terminated in 1973 because of changing circumstances at the political level. It was regrettable because the team had done detailed and methodologically innovative statistical work. She returned to Canada full time in 1977.

Kari Polanyi Levitt believes that, after *Silent Surrender*, her richest contribution is her work about the Caribbean countries during the 1970s. Considering her contribution to the creation of the Plantation Economy Model, conferences, and teaching on the economies of these countries, Kari Polanyi Levitt devoted to the Caribbean her most productive years (Best 2005). In 2008, she received an honorary doctorate from the *University of the West Indies* (Best 2005). The imprint left by Kari Polanyi Levitt in the Caribbean is far reaching, since she helped to build bridges between Canada and the Caribbean. Having affiliations at McGill University and the University of the West Indies, several of her Canadian students went to study in the Caribbean and many students from the region came to study in Canada under her supervision.

For several years, political radicalism was in vogue in the countries of the Caribbean region. The internal divisions, the split of the revolutionary movement in Grenada, and the invasion of the island by the United States in 1983 ended this period. Having lived through these tumultuous years led her to distance herself from radical activism, the path chosen by her mother Ilona.

On the other hand, she followed her father's path, recognizing the role of institutions. From this moment, her contributions attempted to highlight institutional and historical dynamics and their impact on the trajectories of societies. She adopted a vision built on the conviction that

Fig. 3.9 End of 60s, with her sons Tom and Harry

institutions are the best levers for ensuring the protection of populations, their emancipation, and for enabling greater social justice (Fig. 3.9).

References

Best, Lloyd. 2005. 'West Indian from East Europe. Kari Polanyi Levitt.' In *Reclaiming Democracy: The Social Justice and Political Economy of Gregory Baum and Kari Polanyi Levitt*, edited by Marguerite Mendell, 71–91. Montreal: McGill-Queen's University Press.

Best, Lloyd. 2008. 'Kari Levitt—West Indian From East Europe.' In *Lloyd Best: Enduring Relevance of Independent Thought*, edited by Kenneth O. Hall, 57–66. Kingston: Caribbean Freedom.

Girvan, Normand. 2005. Kari Polanyi Levitt and the Theory of Plantation Economy in Contemporary Perspective. In *Reclaiming Democracy: The Social Justice and Political Economy of Gregory Baum and Kari Polanyi Levitt*, edited by Marguerite Mendell, 92–101. Montreal: McGill-Queen's University Press.

Ottawa Privy Council Office. 1968. *Foreign Ownership and the Structure of Canadian Industry: Report of the Task Force on the Structure of Canadian Industry* [aka The Watkins Report].

Polanyi Levitt, Kari. 1968. 'Economic Dependence and Political Disintegration, the case of Canada.' *New World Quarterly* 4 (2).

Polanyi Levitt, Kari. 2003a. 'The Right to Development: Sir Arthur Lewis Memorial Lecture.' *Canadian Journal of Development Studies* 24: 541–555.

Polanyi Levitt, Kari. [1970] 2003b. *Silent Surrender: The Multicorporation in Canada*. Montreal: McGill- Queen's University Press.

Polanyi Levitt, Kari. 2005a. *Reclaiming Development: Independent Thought and Caribbean Community*. Kingston: Ian Randle Publishers.

Polanyi Levitt, Kari. 2005b. 'Confluences.' In *Reclaiming Democracy: The Social Justice and Political Economy of Gregory Baum and Kari Polanyi Levitt*, edited by Marguerite Mendell, 141–166. Montreal: McGill-Queen's University Press.

Polanyi Levitt, Kari. 2005c. 'Globalization, Development and Economics: Reflections on the History of Development Thought.' *Canadian Journal of Development Studies* 26: 517–526.

Polanyi Levitt, Kari, and Lloyd Best. 2009. *Essays on the Theory of the Plantation Economy: A Historical and Institutional Approach to Caribbean Economic Development*. Kingston: University of the West Indies Press.

Ricardo, David. [1817] 2001. *On the Principles of Political Economy and Taxation*. Kitchener: Batoche Books.

Rioux, Michèle, and Hughes Brisson. 2012. 'Interview with Kari Levitt: "Bring the State Back In!".' *Revue Interventions économiques* 45: 12–18. Accessed April 21, 2021. http://interventionseconomiques.revues.org/1686.

Sunkel, Olsvaldo, and Pedro Paz. 1970. *El Subdesarrollo Latinoamericano y la Teoría del Desarrollo*. Mexico: Siglo XXI Editores.

Watkins, Mel. 2005. "The New Canadian Political Economy: Classic and Beyond". In *Reclaiming Democracy: The Social Justice and Political Economy of Gregory Baum and Kari Polanyi Levitt*, edited by Marguerite Mendell, 102–112. Montreal: McGill-Queen's University Press.

CHAPTER 4

The Trajectory of Life Part 3—A Retirement and Her father's Legacy. And Beyond?

Abstract This chapter describes the life and work of Kari Polanyi Levitt from the 1980s on. As the manager of her father's archives, she becomes a major scholar on Karl Polanyi, playing an important role in keeping his memory alive and publishing work that further develops his ideas. In her later body of works, Polanyi Levitt also continues to study development economics and the history of global economics.

Keywords Development Economics · History of Global Economics · Karl Polanyi · International Political Economy

In 1977, Kari Polanyi Levitt returned to full-time teaching at McGill University. She feels "at home" and loves the city, a meeting point for many minorities. She identified herself with its atmosphere (Polanyi Levitt 2005a). From the 1980s, Kari Polanyi Levitt's life followed three axes: (1) teaching at McGill University, (2) frequent research in the Caribbean and (3) the management of her father's archives aimed at keeping his memory alive through the development of the Karl Polanyi Institute at Concordia University.

At a time when economic, social, and human development was disappearing from the agenda of national and international institutions, Polanyi Levitt created a course on development economics at McGill University.

M. Rioux and H. Brisson, *Kari Polanyi Levitt and Canadian Political Economy*, https://doi.org/10.1007/978-3-030-87364-6_4

Fig. 4.1 Kari, Early 1980s

McGill University thus became an important research center on development, with a considerable number of students coming from Third World countries.

Since 1989, when she retired as a professor at McGill University, Kari Polanyi Levitt has written more than ever. From 1989 to 1995, she lectured at the University of the West Indies' Jamaican campus on the theories of economic development. Those years of teaching are dear to her because she developed a multidisciplinary approach to development based on empirical work. Polanyi Levitt also contributed to research organized by the Association of Universities and Colleges of Canada (AUCC) on the state of development studies in Canadian universities in 1985 (Polanyi Levitt 2005b). She was active in research and taking care of the literacy legacy of her father, Karl Polanyi. She was also editor-in-chief of the journal *Caribbean Political Economy* from 1995 to 1997 and worked on the compilation of the writings of George Beckford, published in 2000 (Polanyi Levitt 2000) (Fig. 4.1).

> I grew closer to the West Indies. My most important contribution is probably my work on the Caribbean. I have published [and] edited books on the Caribbean, including the *George Beckford Papers* (2000); *Reclaiming*

Development: Independent Thought and Caribbean Community (2005a), a collection of my essays on Caribbean topics; and with Lloyd Best, *Essays on the Theory of Plantation Economy: a Historical and Institutional Approach to Economic Development* (2009).

Beginning of 1980s

The Legacy of Her Father

When Kari Polanyi Levitt's mother died in 1978, fourteen years after her father's death, she inherited the role of guardian of his legacy. This was the beginning of a new part of her life, which turned out to be fruitful. This role of archivist gave her the opportunity to rediscover the scientific work of her father. It became a dialogue that gave her a new research stimulus.

She acquired a proficiency in Karl Polanyi's ideas while analyzing them in a different light. For several years, this role of ambassador of her father's ideas was confidential or had marginal visibility. When Karl Polanyi's writings gained renewed interest, since the end of the 1990s, this expertise became increasingly valuable.

> I inherited the responsibility of the literary legacy of my father. This added a whole new dimension to my life. In 1986, a centenary conference was organized by the Hungarian Academy of Sciences in Budapest celebrating the life and work of my father. The earthly remains of my parents were transferred from Canada to a cemetery in Budapest.

In 1986, a conference commemorating the centenary of the birth of Karl Polanyi was organized in Budapest to celebrate and recognize the legacy of her father, born in Hungary. Kari Polanyi Levitt was invited to participate in the event. The Hungarian Academy of Sciences, the institutional organizer of the conference, also asked her if she wanted to take advantage of the event to repatriate to Budapest the remains of her parents.

This commemoration of the centenary of the birth of Karl Polanyi had a special resonance in Hungary, as he lived there for several years of his life without having any recognition. Karl Polanyi had to leave the Austro-Hungarian region in 1933 and did not return until thirty years later, when he and his wife published the English translations of great Hungarian poets (Polanyi and Duczynska 1963).[18] The repatriation of the remains of Karl Polanyi and Ilona Duczynska was perceived in Hungary as a return of two great forgotten figures of the country (Fig. 4.2).

Kari Polanyi Levitt was deeply touched by this experience – feeling it as a true homecoming – of rediscovery of her Hungarian and European roots. She realized that her father's identity was multicultural. Yet, Karl Polanyi's Hungarian roots remained so central that she claimed that everything he had written stemmed from this Hungarian connection. Although she has never learned to speak Hungarian or lived in the country, Kari Polanyi Levitt has been marked by a Hungarian intellectual heritage and roots, as several of her colleagues and friends have pointed out (Best 2005; Mendell 2005).

Her father became an important influence for her, even though other economists had a great resonance with her work as well. She said:

> I refuse to take labels. If I would have to choose the one thinker I have really learned the most from, Marx would be there, along with Keynes and

Fig. 4.2 Kari when the ashes of her parents were returned to Budapest, 1983

> Schumpeter. Marx, Schumpeter, and Keynes are the great ones. Keynes is a giant and I am sorry I did not have the chance to meet him, even when I was in Cambridge for two years. My father never met him either. I knew Joan Robinson very well, who was involved with him. She was a family friend who visited in Montreal many times. If I had to choose only one book to take to my grave – what a terrible question to ask because I'm supposed to say the Holy Bible [laughs] –I would take my father's *The Great Transformation* [1945].

She knew and often discussed this book with her father, but it took time for her to understand its importance. The book followed the lectures he gave in England – the evening classes he gave to the *Worker's Educational Association.* The first two chapters, about international affairs in the 1920s and the 1930s, were familiar to her as it was everything she and her father had talked about. It was part of her. Yet, Kari Polanyi Levitt did not understand the importance of the book because her father was concerned with archaic and primitive societies when he was at Columbia University, from 1947 until his death. Why was her father interested in ancient civilizations and primitive societies? It took to understood how it all fitted together. These societies were different from ours in the sense that their economy was embedded in their social institutions. Capitalism was not.

> It is only in capitalism, or market society he called it, that the relations are turned upside-down, and the economy rules over the politics, over the ideologies, over the religion and over anything else. It becomes the driving force and the most important aspect of everything. This is what he called the "dis-embedding of the economy.

Kari Polanyi Levitt believes the difference between Marx and her father is not great. She thinks Polanyi owes to Marx, depending on how you read Marx. When Marx talked of commodities that are moving around, he talked of the human relations behind those making the commodities and those making the inputs. In the division of labor, even on an international scale, the underlying social relations are important. This is similar to her father's point about how economic laws governing the movements of commodities in the market also govern our lives.

She concludes that there is an alienation theme in Marx – both explicit and implicit – which also runs deep in Polanyi.

> In Marx, you have a certain economic determinism based on the forces of production, and from that he builds the rest of the society. In a sense, my father differs from Marx. But there are things in Marx that have definitely influenced my father and I do think that my father was the Marx of the 20th Century.

At the initiative of Margie Mendell of Concordia University, the *Karl Polanyi Institute of Political Economy* was created in 1988 where Kari Polanyi Levitt deposited all her father's writings. She became associated with the Karl Polanyi Institute at Concordia University, of which she is the honorary president. The growing interest in her father is significant. *Arte Network* listed him as one of the economists for a series on capitalism, the list of economists includes Smith, Marx, Keynes, and Schumpeter (Dale 2010, 2015, 2016).

> This would have been unthinkable five years ago. I would have been very surprised to see my father mentioned with the great figures of economics. That has a lot to do with what is going on in the world.

And Beyond

Kari Polanyi Levitt devoted most of her work to the study of development economics. She came to think that colonialism constituted a fundamental aspect of global capitalism, both in its contemporary and past forms. She recalled her father's theory that nineteenth-century capitalism represented a rupture in the history of humanity by placing the market at the center of social life.

His explanation focused on the emergence of four capitalist institutions during the nineteenth century: the balance of power among European countries, the international gold standard, a self- regulating market, and the constitutional state. Kari Polanyi Levitt added colonialism to these four institutions.

Both hers and her father work emphasize the importance of collective action and institutions. According to Karl Polanyi, the economy is not an independent entity, but rather the articulation of various institutional processes generating different models according to arrangements of market exchanges, redistribution, and reciprocity.

The economy originates from the dependence on nature and the collectivity for survival (Polanyi 2008, 53). This definition allows for the observation of all forms of exchange as means to support the people. Economic relationships are historically embedded in other forms of social relationships. The separation of economic relationships from other types of relationship is peculiar to capitalism or the "market society." Such a broad view opens the door to take into consideration cultural traits likely to have an impact on economic life. However, these aspects are usually omitted from orthodox economics.

Kari Polanyi Levitt followed her father, as she studied institutions, principles, standards, and values in political economy. In a recent book, *From the Great Transformation to the Great Financialization: On Karl Polanyi and Other Essays* (2013), she proposed a historical approach to the capitalist system and the transformation of power relations between the West and developing countries. She argued that the West was slowly losing its influence over the latter. She analyzed the financialization process, the tendency of companies to transfer their assets from the production sector to the financial sector. This involves taking resources from the hands of producers and taxpayers for the benefits of individuals or institutions holding financial assets.

This process results in the reduction of economic value to a simple financial value exchangeable on the markets in the form of securities. This means that finance is independent from production. Therefore, capital markets have lost their primary function, which was to assess the long-term viability of different firms. According to Polanyi Levitt, this phenomenon appeared when the value of the stock became the standard for evaluating the performance of firms (Polanyi Levitt 2008). It has been more intense in Great Britain and the United States, where gains in the financial markets have contributed disproportionately to the increase in Gross Domestic Product (GDP), while the industrial sector was shrinking. As the share of the industrial sector on GDP decreases, that of finance, insurance, and real estate increases (Polanyi Levitt 2013).

Financialization is characterized as the ability, on the part of financial capital, to gain the upper hand over all commercial and industrial activities. It stems from a recurrent overaccumulation of capital and is contributing to the increase in income inequality and the concentration of wealth in the hands of a minority on a global scale. Polanyi Levitt pointed out that the 2008 crisis demonstrated that the countries at the center of the world economy can also be badly affected (Polanyi Levitt 2008).

For the past few years, Kari Polanyi Levitt also devoted her research time to the history of economic thoughts. She divided the expansion of capitalism over the past five hundred years into three waves.

- The first wave was that of mercantilism, running from 1500 to 1800.
- The second wave corresponded to the creation of a world economy in the nineteenth century, until the First World War.
- From the economic crisis of the 1930s, a third wave took shape, that of the counterrevolution of capital, marked by a desire to reduce the earnings obtained by workers (Polanyi Levitt 2008).

This broad historical perspective on capitalism leads her to observe the evolution of North–South relations of domination and dependency, as well as the changing organization of the global economy, which is shifting from West to East (from Europe and the United States to Asia). The idea of mutually beneficial relationship between MNCs and governments of the MNCs' countries of origin is reminiscent of the relationship that united monarchs and chartered companies in the days of mercantilism (Polanyi Levitt 2008). Mercantilism was centered on conquest and the exploitation of trade inequalities. This mercantilist historical heritage still structures the dynamics of the global economy and revolves around the separation between the centers and the peripheries; the centers controlling distribution, finance, communications, and access to technology whereas the peripheries export raw materials and non-technologically intensive manufactured goods.

Has globalization gone too far? Kari Polanyi Levitt believes that intervention and regulation must be elaborated and implemented at the national level and that any types of global governance schemes would be introduced primarily to benefit the banks and MNCs. She argues that the ***national state*** must be "freed" from the ***transnational*** rather than the other way around.

> States are the only actors capable of stopping the destructive tsunami of global capital. The Nation-State is the only space where people can exercise political power. A global constitution is unrealistic. Any effort in that direction is simply going to strengthen the hold of the multinationals because of the inequalities of power. The only institution through which we could plan and socialize the multinationals is the Nation-State; they have not failed, they simply have not tried.

Nation-states can enact laws and enforce them. It is where politics can happen, in the sense of power relations between the different classes and interests within a society.

> The price for managing your economy with democracy with some equity and social programs is to limit the freedom of foreign money to come and go, in other words to keep out foreign capital. That turns on its head all the general beliefs about development. Bresser-Pereira, with a new developmentalist approach, argued that in Latin America, the issue is no more the need to industrialize, it is a case of managing and controlling economies in a way that benefits people.

Kari Polanyi Levitt is finishing a manuscript on development economics from mercantilism to now discussing the rising importance of the Global South and the shift in geopolitical power relations.

> In my coming book on development economics, I note Prebisch had a great influence in the 1950s. In the 1960s, came the critics, from the right and from the left. The right produced the neo-liberal counter-revolution. On the left, there were criticisms of Prebisch and his theory because it was too statist or dependent on foreign investments. The next generation the scholars, including Sunkel, were critical of his import substitution model depending on foreign investments. Prebisch and Lewis were important. It is possible to rebuild on the basis of their work and thus is the goal of the "new developmentalism" and of its architect, Luiz Carlos Bresser-Pereira.

References

Best, Lloyd. 2005. 'West Indian from East Europe. Kari Polanyi Levitt.' In *Reclaiming Democracy: The Social Justice and Political Economy of Gregory Baum and Kari Polanyi Levitt*, 71–91. Edited by Marguerite Mendell. Montreal: McGill-Queen's University Press.

Dale,Gareth. 2010. *Karl Polanyi: The Limits of The Market*. Cambridge: Polity Press.

Dale, Gareth. 2015. *Karl Polanyi: The Hungarian Writings*. Manchester: Manchester University Press.

Dale, Gareth. 2016. *Karl Polanyi: A Life on the Left*. New York: Columbia University Press.

Mendell, Marguerite. 2005. *Reclaiming Democracy: The Social Justice and Political Economy of Gregory Baum and Kari Polanyi Levitt*. Montreal: McGill-Queen's University Press.

Polanyi Levitt, Kari, and Lloyd Best. 2009. *Essays on the Theory of the Plantation Economy: A Historical and Institutional Approach to Caribbean Economic Development*. Kingston: University of the West Indies Press.

Polanyi Levitt, Kari. 2000. *The George Beckford Papers, Selected and Introduced by Kari Levitt*. Kingston: University of the West Indies Press.

Polanyi Levitt, Kari. 2005a. *Reclaiming Development: Independent Thought and Caribbean Community*. Kingston: Ian Randle Publishers.

Polanyi Levitt, Kari. 2005b. 'Globalization, Development and Economics: Reflections on the History of Development Thought.' *Canadian Journal of Development Studies* 26: 517–526.

Polanyi Levitt, Kari. 2013. *From the Great Transformation to the Great Financialization: On Karl Polanyi and Other Essays*. Halifax: Fernwood Publishing.

Polanyi, Karl, and Ilona Duczynska. 1963. *The Plough and the Pen, Writings from Hungary, 1930–1956*. Toronto: McClelland and Stewart.

Polanyi, Karl. 2008. 'L'économie en tant que processus institutionnalisé.' In *Essais de Karl Polanyi*, 53–77. Edited by Michele Cangiani and Jérôme. Maucourant. Paris: Seuil.

CHAPTER 5

Conclusion

Abstract Kari's diverse background tells the story of the emergence of a global citizen. Kari Polanyi Levitt had a critical mind and a militant life in many respects. Her unique trajectory has at its core the desire to fight for social justice. Her work is deeply rooted in the belief that economics can provide the right tools to ensure that globalization benefits the many instead of the few.

Keywords Globalization · Social justice · International political economy · Canadian economist

Kari's diverse background, including her childhood in Red Vienna, her education in England, and her professional life in Canada and the Caribbean, tells a story of the emergence of a global citizen (Figs. 5.1 and 5.2).

The reference to a global village is not trivial. Kari's work is tinged with this sense of duty to contribute to the construction of this global society, a quest for social forces that make it possible to contain and control the current phenomenon of the globalization of capitalism.

Having grown up in a socialist home, she had a sense of duty, self-giving and, above all, a desire to contribute. This is how her path was traced, driven by the need to put critical thinking at the service of a

M. Rioux and H. Brisson, *Kari Polanyi Levitt and Canadian Political Economy*, https://doi.org/10.1007/978-3-030-87364-6_5

Fig. 5.1 Kari in Haiti, 1986

Fig. 5.2 Kari at her Book Launch, University of Jamaica, 2010

commitment to social empowerment. This unique trajectory has at its core the desire to fight for social justice.

Throughout her career, she has looked at statistics as tools. Her solid experience in this area equipped her well to criticize the most common uses of statistics. Her statistical nous allowed her to capture the aspects of life in society that institutions reflect, and therefore how statistical measures do not take them properly into consideration. On the basis of this knowledge of statistics, she made her debut and built her scientific credibility and scientific career. Her statistical studies in the Atlantic region became invaluable for the design of development policies for the region. Several of these figures, compiled for the first time by Kari, have been compiled on a regular basis ever since. Therefore, she helped to unveil this region to the world, to give it a face, and to help those who want to better understand it. She did the same in understanding the specific historical social and economic development of Canada and the Caribbean region.

Kari Polanyi Levitt had a critical mind and a militant life in many respects. Her work is deeply rooted in the belief that economics can aspire to the status of science, rather than a simple "soft" science serving ideologies. From this point of view, globalization, for example, is not "neoliberal" or "alter-globalist," "leftist" or "rightist." Globalization exists, and statistics prove it. For her, economics allows us to better understand such a phenomenon and the development of statistical tools allows us to measure it. With these measurement tools, it is possible to develop our analytical tools and mechanisms of intervention to ensure that globalization takes place for the common good.

Wishing to safeguard her scientific independence, she never approached power circles. She is also independent in theoretical terms, based on a profound knowledge of economic thoughts and history of the capitalist system. Her education and career were shaped by the ideas of Marx, Keynes, and Polanyi among many others. She was inscribed in a left-leaning militant perspective that was critical of the market economy and globalization. Her family and education, the attraction of her parents towards the USSR, the experience of social life in workers' and trade union circles, her East European origins, and years of life in Europe where several ideologies coexisted, all had a considerable impact on her social activism. Kari Polanyi Levitt's conviction in the relevance of institutions was gradually confirmed as her aversion to radical forms of militancy took shape. Her rejection of radical militancy came when she witnessed the extreme polarization of political debate in the young Caribbean states. The violence engendered by the Caribbean revolutionary movement distanced her from activism, a distance which had already appeared several years before in reaction to the severe Soviet repression of the Budapest revolution in 1956. The radicalization of the revolutionary movement in the Caribbean countries made her realize the gap separating her from radical militants who wanted the destruction of institutions. She adopted a resolutely assumed institutionalist perspective, aware that institutions can serve to protect populations against all forms of excess committed by the powers in place. She believed that interventions and policies at the national level are the best remedy against globalization, which has gone too far.

Since the early 2000s, her eyesight has diminished. This handicap prevents her from reading – but not from thinking. At 97, she still studies political economy and remains on the lookout for interesting readings with the help of technology. She frequently attends cultural events and her social life continues to be filled with meetings with friends of all ages and from all backgrounds. Certainly, such interest in system transformations is not trivial for an intellectual who has the conviction that institutions can mediate changes and improve the well-being of people.

This book is a tribute to a great Canadian economist that will be remembered for many years to come. Her life and work can help to understand the scientific and political challenges that humanity faces and the incredible impacts of globalization in its diverse manifestations, including the current pandemic of Covid-19.

Her message is simple, yet very demanding. She wishes that we think about the way we live in this world, reconsider our place in the universe, and our relationship with nature. For her, the solution does not lie in ever more sophisticated technologies; on the contrary, it lies in questioning how we really want to live with each other, while also considering the environment that we are destroying. Kari Polanyi Levitt was and is still driven by a humanist ideal, her outlook on life being global and people oriented, and trying to find a way to re-embed the economy in the wider social system. She was awarded the Order of Canada in 2014.

> For her contributions to the establishment of international development studies as an interdisciplinary academic field, and for her research on political economy in the Caribbean. Kari Polanyi Levitt helped establish international development as a field of academic study in Canada. A

professor of economics at McGill University since the early 1960s, she was also a founding member of the Canadian Association for the Study of International Development. Her analysis of the expansion of multinational corporations in Canada sparked widespread debate among experts in the field of economics, and her extensive knowledge of the economic systems of Caribbean countries has made her a sought-after adviser to national governments and development organizations. (See: https://www.gg.ca/en/honours/recipients/146-10948)

Postface

I was 19 years old. She was brilliant. I had come to McGill to study languages. She was immersed in things Caribbean, and I timidly stepped on for the ride. I ended up studying economics as her graduate student, with a clear focus on the Caribbean and Kari deeply embedded in my back pocket. Through Kari, I understood the specific and very precious hybridity of the Caribbean, of my Caribbean. Through Kari, I learned that committing to the cause also meant running out of gas on the highway at 2am on route from Ottawa to Montreal during the time of the Grenada invasion.

The memories are numerous and not surprisingly, still continue to accumulate. I am now almost 60, and Kari is still brilliant! It seems hard to imagine that I have now known her for over 40 years and that our lives have become so intimately intertwined. She met me as a "baby-thinker," reassuring my parents that their teenage daughter would be fine in big-city Montreal. She welcomed them into her home on numerous occasions and made them know that the Caribbean hospitality and sense of extended family that they had known, also lived at 250 St Anne's Rd in St Anne de Bellevue. I wrote my Master's thesis from the second-floor bedroom of the rambling old house that we all knew as Kari's; I would never have finished it without her heart and hearth. I worked on her Macintosh computer and saved my writing on floppy disks. In my

M. Rioux and H. Brisson, *Kari Polanyi Levitt and Canadian Political Economy*, https://doi.org/10.1007/978-3-030-87364-6

naïveté, I even contemplated taking on the name Polanyi if I continued in academia, because I knew that Kari was the last of her line. Countless evenings of copious wine, "plenty food," and fly-size mosquitoes on the veranda of the house in St Anne are a warm smile for me. Kari in her garden, trees planted for lost loved ones....

My MA completed, Kari was the first to adamantly encourage me to step as far away as I could from the ivory tower that was the university. My professional dance career ended up taking place in Europe, so Kari was only able to see me perform for the first (and only) time in April 2019! "I didn't understand anything," she said, "where's the story?" I told her that contemporary dance didn't necessarily have a clear narrative. She did the dismissive Kari shrug, smilingly grabbed my arm in a tight hug, and said, "I'm just so happy to see you dance!" I knew she was deeply proud.

Some twenty years after taking her advice and following my dream, I was in Montreal for a visit and Kari said, "Angel, I want you to come home. It's time for you to come home. Montreal is not such a bad place, you know..." I proposed that we buy a place together so that she would have the presence and support of my family close by. That was dismissed, of course. Company was welcome—even constant company!—but anything that could be even remotely construed as a loss of autonomy was flatly rejected. When I and my family first arrived in July 2014, we camped out with Kari for the first two weeks. My son was 10 years old at the time and, one evening, as we were getting back to the apartment after a day of buying beds and other such comforts, Kari was stepping out. It was 9 pm. My son asked her where she was going, "I'm going to listen to some music with a friend in a café." With consternation, my son declared, "But you're already 90 years old!" Kari's response before sauntering off was, "Yes, but I'm not deaf!".

Now entrusted with all of her worldly possessions, negotiations, and fantasies, I watch her simply live longer rather than grow old, more interested in diving into one of Piketty's voluminous marvels than in any conversation about love, life, death, or leaving this Earth. Kari cannot imagine ever coming to an end. Fiercely insistent on living on her own until her recent health setbacks, she now relies totally on others for her well-being and loudly hates every bit of it. She sees herself as she needs to—independent, interested, involved, nimbly hopping from her beloved Trinidad to her Austrian homeland and back to the place where her sons are, Montreal—always surrounded by friends and thinkers, thinkers and friends, near and far. The challenge to find miracles for Kari is constantly present for the small band of elves and fairies that now surround her. And miracles we do make.

Singularly uninterested in having anything about this journey come to a close, Kari seems like an unstoppable force, defying the limits of the body and glorifying the power of the fighting spirit. A couple months after suffering a massive stroke at the end of 2019, Kari said to me, "And all those people who thought I wasn't going to make it, well, they don't know me!" As if we can really choose.... I suppose if anyone could, Kari would be the one.

As long as Piketty and Polanyi can continue to be in dialogue, Kari's world will be alright. At 98, and by no means out of steam, she defies us all with her steadfastness and stubborn perseverance, her sharp wit and intellectual alacrity. Undaunted by her wheelchair and the orchestration required (elegantly performed by the elves and fairies of course), the new normal is a zoom call with her friends to celebrate her birthday. There's barely enough time in the two-hour call to give each of the over 100 attendees the chance to extend their birthday wishes to Kari—and she loves it! In spite of being a staunch atheist, she even managed to get a letter and a rosary from Pope Francis for her 97th!! Kari asks, and she divinely receives.

Kari has been to me what few have managed: mentor, friend, provocateur, longstanding, unconditional, and crazy-making. My world would have been incomplete without her. Somehow, I have become the daughter she never had. I am honored, grateful, humbled that this brilliant mind and absolute lover of life would choose me for that role. I always thought she would have relied on one of those who hadn't left, on one of those who shared and nurtured her intellectual interests, whether related to the Caribbean or, more recently, to her post-retirement passion, which was the work of her beloved father and equally extraordinary thinker, Karl Polanyi. She has worked with unwavering conviction since her retirement from McGill to promote the work of her father, in all of its current pertinence. In spite of some of us, her semi-paralysis and her loss of sight, Kari continues to negotiate publishing contracts and write articles and conference papers! As she has pointed out on several occasions, if she were to stop, that's what would kill her.

Whatever Kari is to me, I know she has an equally generous place in hearts and minds all over the globe. This publication is a gift that honors an extraordinary thinker, teacher, friend. Her legacy will live on in the Karl and Kari Polanyi Foundation, which will be run by elves and fairies of course, but only once La Levitt is gone. And there's no telling when that might be—it's certainly not in her plans!

Angélique Willkie
Montreal, May 30, 2021

Timeline

1923	Birth of Kari Polanyi
1934	Arrives in London
1941	Studies at the London School of Economics
1943–1945	Interrupts her studies for military service at the Office of Research of the Amalgamated Engineering Union, London
1945	Resumes studies at the London School of Economics
1946	Works with of Nicholas Kaldor on the effects of Allied bombings
1947	Graduates from the London School of Economics, specializing in statistics

1947	Arrives in Canada, to reunite with Joseph Levitt
1948	Works at the Acme Screw and Gear Company, and gets involved the Union of Automobile Workers
1950	Marriage to Joseph Levitt in Toronto
Early 1950–1956	Worked as an editor for the United Electrical Workers, the Mine's union journal, the Mill and Smelter Workers Union
1956	Quits the Communist Party
1957–1959	Master's Degree in Economics, University of Toronto
1959	Begins PhD studies in economics, University of Toronto
1960	First stay in Jamaica, to assist Burton Kearstead in his research work

(continued)

M. Rioux and H. Brisson, *Kari Polanyi Levitt and Canadian Political Economy*, https://doi.org/10.1007/978-3-030-87364-6

(continued)

1961	Arrival in Montreal: position of professor at McGill University
1961	Second stay in the Caribbean (Jamaica and Trinidad)
1964	Death of her father Karl Polanyi
1965–1975	Directs a project of research on the economy of the Maritime provinces with Statistics Canada
1966–1968	Directs, with Lloyd Best, a project of research on the development and industrialization of the Caribbean at McGill's Center for Developing-Area Studies
1968	Publication of an article in the *New World Quarterly*, which will be at the core of *Silent Surrender*
1969–1973	Moves with her family in Trinidad to set up of a system National of Statistics
1971	Publication of the first edition of *Silent Surrender*
1970	Meeting in Hamburg organized by Osvaldo Sunkel where she meets several researchers working on the economy of developing countries
1974–1977	Accepts a position as visiting professor at the University of the West Indies
1977	Back in Montreal, resumes her work as full professor at McGill University
1978	By following the death of her mother Ilona Duczynska, becomes responsible for the archives of Karl Polanyi
1980	Plays a role in the creation of the Canadian Association for the Study of International Development

1982	Leads a research project, together with Ayse Bugra Trak on the status development studies in Canada
1982	Writes a report on Canadian policy in the Caribbean for the Department of Foreign Affairs of Canada
1986	Commemorates the centenary of Karl Polanyi in Budapest with there patriation of the remains of Karl Polanyi and Ilona Duczynska
1988	Margie Mendell launches the Karl Polanyi Institute at Concordia University
1989–1992	Retirement as professor from McGill University, becomes Professor Emeritus
2002	Resumes the work begun with Lloyd Best on the plantation economy in order to publish it
2003	Publication of the second edition of *Silent Surrender*
2004	Conference in Hamburg in her honor, during which she is made Honorary member of the Hungarian Academy of Science
2005	Publishes *Reclaiming Development: Independent Thought and Caribbean Community*, a compilation of articles and conferences from previous years

(continued)

(continued)

2005	Publication of *Reclaiming Democracy: The Social Justice and Political Economy of Gregory Baum and Kari Polanyi Levitt*, a collective work edited by Margie Mendell
2008	Receives the John Kenneth Galbraith prize from the Progressive Economics Forum
2008	Receives an honorary doctorate from the University of the West Indies
2009	Publication of *Essays on the Theory of Plantation Economy*, which brings together her work and that of Lloyd Best on the plantation economy model
2013	At 90, she publishes *From the Great Transformation to the Great Financialization*

Bibliography

Best, Lloyd. 2005. 'West Indian from East Europe. Kari Polanyi Levitt.' In *Reclaiming Democracy: The Social Justice and Political Economy of Gregory Baum and Kari Polanyi Levitt*, edited by Marguerite Mendell, 71–91. Montreal: McGill-Queen's University Press.

Best, Lloyd. 2008. 'Kari Levitt – West Indian From East Europe.' In *Lloyd Best: Enduring Relevance of Independent Thought*, edited by Kenneth O. Hall, 57–66. Kingston: Caribbean Freedom.

British Bombing Survey Unit. 1945–1947. *Nicholas Kaldor's German War Economy Papers*, SZ/BBSU/103.

Cameron, Duncan. 2005. 'Epilogue.' In *Reclaiming Democracy: The Social Justice and Political Economy of Gregory Baum and Kari Polanyi Levitt*, edited by Marguerite Mendell, 167–174. Montreal: McGill-Queen's University Press.

Clancier, Philippe, Francis Joannès, Pierre Rouillard and Aline Tenu. 2005. *Autour de Polanyi: Vocabulaires, théories et modalités des échanges*. Paris: De Boccard.

Dale,Gareth. 2010. *Karl Polanyi: The Limits of The Market*. Cambridge: Polity Press.

Dale, Gareth. 2015. *Karl Polanyi: The Hungarian Writings*. Manchester: Manchester University Press.

Dale, Gareth. 2016. *Karl Polanyi: A Life on the Left*. New York: Columbia University Press.

Furtado,Celso. 1963. *The Economic Growth of Brazil*. Los Angeles: University of California Press.

M. Rioux and H. Brisson, *Kari Polanyi Levitt and Canadian Political Economy*, https://doi.org/10.1007/978-3-030-87364-6

Girvan, Normand. 2005. Kari Polanyi Levitt and the Theory of Plantation Economy in Contemporary Perspective'. In *Reclaiming Democracy: The Social Justice and Political Economy of Gregory Baum and Kari Polanyi Levitt*, edited by Marguerite Mendell, 92–101. Montreal: McGill-Queen's University Press.

Hicks, John R. 1952. *The Social Framework: An Introduction to Economics*. Oxford: Clarendon Press.

Hobsbawm, Eric. 1999. *Industry and Empire: From 1750 to the Present Day*. New York: The New Press.

Kaldor, Nicholas. 1945. 'The German War Economy.' *The Review of Economic Studies* 13: 33–52.

Kapp, Yvonne. 1977. *Eleanor Marx*. New York: Pantheon Books.

Mendell, Marguerite. 2005. *Reclaiming Democracy: The Social Justice and Political Economy of Gregory Baum and Kari Polanyi Levitt*. Montreal: McGill-Queen's University Press.

Maucourant, Jérôme. 2011. *Avez-vous lu Polanyi?* Paris: Flammarion.

Maucourant, Jérôme, and Sébastien Plociniczak. 2011. 'Penser l'institution et le marché avec Karl Polanyi; Contre la crise (de la pensée) économique.' *Revue de la régulation* 10. Accessed April 21, 2021. http://regulation.revues.org/9439.

Ottawa Privy Council Office. 1968. *Foreign Ownership and the Structure of Canadian Industry: Report of the Task Force on the Structure of Canadian Industry* [aka The Watkins Report].

Polanyi Levitt, Kari. 1967. *Canada-West Indies Economic Relations*. Montreal: Montreal Private Planning Association of Canada, Canadian Trade Committee.

Polanyi Levitt, Kari. 1968. 'Economic Dependence and Political Disintegration, the Case of Canada.' *New World Quarterly* 4 (2).

Polanyi Levitt, Kari. 1978. *La capitulation tranquille: les multinationales, pouvoir parallèle?* Montreal: L'Étincelle.

Polanyi Levitt, Kari. 1985. 'The Origins and Implications of the Caribbean Basin Initiative Mortgaging Sovereignty?' *International Journal* 40: 229–281.

Polanyi Levitt, Kari. 1990a. *The Life and Work of Karl Polanyi*. Montreal: Black Rose Books.

Polanyi Levitt, Kari. 1990b. 'Debt, Adjustment and Development: Looking to the 1990s.' *Economic and Political Weekly* 25: 1585–1594.

Polanyi Levitt, Kari. 1992. 'IMF Structural Adjustment: Short-Term Gain for Long-Term Pain?' *Economic and Political Weekly* 27: 97–102.

Polanyi Levitt, Kari. 2000. *The George Beckford Papers, Selected and Introduced by Kari Levitt*. Kingston: University of the West Indies Press.

Polanyi Levitt, Karl. [1944] 2001. *The Great Transformation*. Boston: Beacon Press.

Polanyi Levitt, Kari. 2003a. 'The Right to Development: Sir Arthur Lewis Memorial Lecture.' *Canadian Journal of Development Studies* 24: 541–555.

Polanyi Levitt, Kari. [1970] 2003b. *Silent Surrender: The Multicorporation in Canada*. Montreal: McGill-Queen's University Press.

Polanyi Levitt, Kari. 2004a. 'Independent Thought and Caribbean Community.' *Canadian Journal of Development Studies* 25: 225–237.

Polanyi Levitt, Kari. 2004b. 'Development and Regionalism: Karl Polanyi's Ideas and the Contemporary World System.' Lecture given during the Conference *Karl Polanyi's Ideas and the Contemporary World System*, Budapest, November 2004.

Polanyi Levitt, Kari. 2005a. *Reclaiming Development: Independent Thought and Caribbean Community*. Kingston: Ian Randle Publishers.

Polanyi Levitt, Kari. 2005b. 'Confluences.' In *Reclaiming Democracy: The Social Justice and Political Economy of Gregory Baum and Kari Polanyi Levitt*, edited by Marguerite Mendell, 141–166. Montreal: McGill-Queen's University Press.

Polanyi Levitt, Kari. 2005c. 'Globalization, Development and Economics: Reflections on the History of Development Thought.' *Canadian Journal of Development Studies* 26: 517–526.

Polanyi Levitt, Kari. 2006a. 'Reclaiming Policy Space for Equitable Economic Development.' Lecture given for the North South Institute, Ottawa, January 2006. Accessed April 21, 2021. http://www.nsi-ins.ca/upload/levitt_jan_06_reclaiming_policy_space.pdf.

Polanyi Levitt, Kari. 2006b. 'Keynes and Polanyi: the 1920s and the 1990s.' *Review of International Political Economy* 13 (1): 152.

Polanyi Levitt, Karl. 2008a. 'L'économie en tant que processus institutionnalisé.' In *Essais de Karl Polanyi*, edited by Michele Cangiani and Jérôme, 53–77. Maucourant. Paris: Seuil.

Polanyi Levitt, Kari. 2008b. 'The Great Financialization.' Kari Levitt's John Kenneth Galbraith Lecture, Progressive Economics Forum, September 22nd, 2008. Accessed April 21, 2021. http://www.progressive-economics.ca/2008/09/22/kari-levitts-jkg-lecture/.

Polanyi Levitt, Kari. 2012. 'The Power of Ideas: Keynes, Hayek and Polanyi.' *International Journal of Political Economy* 41: 5–15.

Polanyi Levitt, Kari. 2013. *From the Great Transformation to the Great Financialization: On Karl Polanyi and Other Essays*. Halifax: Fernwood Publishing.

Polanyi Levitt, Kari and Cherita Girvan. 1970. 'The Old Mercantilism and the New: A Canadian Perspective.' *Social and Economic Studies* 19: 466–489.

Polanyi Levitt, Kari, and Ilona Duczynska. 1963. *The Plough and the Pen, Writings from Hungary, 1930–1956*. Toronto: McClelland and Stewart.

Polanyi Levitt, Kari, and Iqbal Gulati. 1970. 'Income Effect of Tourism Spending: Mystification Multiplied; A Critical Comment on the Zinder Report.' *Social and Economic Studies* 19: 326–343.

PolanyiLevitt, Kari, and Kenneth McRobbie (eds.). 2000. *Karl Polanyi in Vienna: The Contemporary Significance of the Great Transformation*. Montreal, Canada: Black Rose Books.

Polanyi Levitt, Kari, and Lloyd Best. 2009. *Essays on the Theory of the Plantation Economy: A Historical and Institutional Approach to Caribbean Economic Development*. Kingston: University of the West Indies Press.

Polanyi Levitt, Kari, and Michael Witter. 1996. *The Critical Tradition of Caribbean Political Economy*. Kingston: Ian Randle Publishers.

Prebisch, Raúl. 1950. *The Economic Development of Latin America and its Principal Problems*. New York: United Nations Department of Economic Affairs.

Prebisch, Raúl. 1959. 'Commercial Policy in the Underdevelopped Countries.' *American Economic Review* 49: 251–273.

Ricardo, David. [1817] 2001. *On the Principles of Political Economy and Taxation*. Kitchener: Batoche Books.

Rioux, Michèle, and Hughes Brisson. 2012. 'Interview with Kari Levitt: "Bring the State Back In!".' *Revue Interventions économiques* 45: 12–18. Accessed April 21, 2021. http://interventionseconomiques.revues.org/1686.

Sunkel, Olsvaldo, and Pedro Paz. 1970. *El Subdesarrollo Latinoamericano y la Teoría del Desarrollo*. Mexico: Siglo XXI Editores.

Watkins, Mel. 2005. 'The New Canadian Political Economy: Classic and Beyond'. In *Reclaiming Democracy: The Social Justice and Political Economy of Gregory Baum and Kari Polanyi Levitt*, edited by Marguerite Mendell, 102–112. Montreal: McGill-Queen's University Press.

The manufacturer's authorised representative in the EU is Springer Nature Customer Service Centre GmbH, Europaplatz 3, 69115 Heidelberg, Germany. If you have any concerns regarding our products, please contact ProductSafety@springernature.com

Printed and bound by CPI Group (UK) Ltd, Croydon, CR0 4YY

30/09/2026

02225472-0001